Urban Rail Transit English

城市轨道交通实用英语

杨 茜 李 玲 主编

化学工业出版社

·北京·

内容简介

本书为高校城市轨道交通专业教材，内容包括城市轨道交通文化、票务、站点信息、出入闸口、车站安全、站台候车、突发情况应急反应、国外城市轨道交通纵览、城市轨道交通管理、城市轨道交通法律法规等十章内容。本书知识点新颖全面，同时配套外教朗读音频，可作为专业基础课教材和相关从业人员参考书使用。

图书在版编目（CIP）数据

城市轨道交通实用英语/杨茜，李玲主编. —北京：
化学工业出版社，2021.8
ISBN 978-7-122-39406-4

Ⅰ.①城… Ⅱ.①杨… ②李… Ⅲ.①城市铁路-轨道
交通-英语-高等职业教育-教材 Ⅳ.①U239.5

中国版本图书馆CIP数据核字（2021）第127962号

责任编辑：王　可　蔡洪伟　王　芳	文字编辑：李　曦　林　丹
责任校对：宋　玮	装帧设计：张　辉

出版发行：化学工业出版社（北京市东城区青年湖南街13号　邮政编码100011）
印　　刷：北京云浩印刷有限责任公司
装　　订：三河市振勇印装有限公司
787mm×1092mm　1/16　印张11¾　字数283千字　2023年5月北京第1版第1次印刷

购书咨询：010-64518888　　　　　　　　　售后服务：010-64518899
网　　址：http://www.cip.com.cn

凡购买本书，如有缺损质量问题，本社销售中心负责调换。

定　　价：38.00元　　　　　　　　　　　　　　　　　　　　　　版权所有　违者必究

编写人员名单

主　编　杨　茜　李　玲

副主编　杨　蓓　吴　虹　钟炳芳

参　编　王　倩　刘　颖　郭粒粒　周怡乔　杜　薇　刘　海
　　　　　高　婧　潘　薇　赵雅婷　罗惠扬　李雪婷　牛晓丹

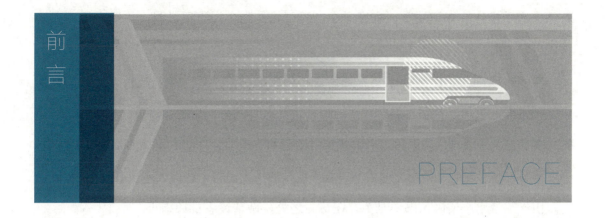

前言 PREFACE

随着中国城市化进程的加快，城市规模不断扩大，城市向周边辐射面越来越宽，交通问题已经是城市发展的主要问题。加快轨道交通建设，有助于大大缓解交通压力，为人民提供便利的交通方式，同时可以减少城市的交通污染排放。另外，中国城市的国际化程度日益提高，对外文化交流活动愈发频繁，吸引着越来越多的海外游客到中国旅游。基于此，各服务行业从业人员的国际化服务水平和服务意识都需要进一步提高。由此，提高从事轨道交通和相关服务行业的本专科学生和管理人员的专业英语口语能力和英语阅读能力的要求越发迫切。

然而现有环境下地铁客服人员还是主要使用中文服务，对于客服所必需的安检服务、安全提示、乘车服务、应急情况等英语表达捉襟见肘。一般的客服人员几乎不会英语表达，英语能力较强的人员也只能应答较简单的对话。本书弥补了地铁专业英语方面的不足，同时使用大量的案例分析和场景对话让学生能够轻松掌握地铁英语主要内容，大量的海外地铁英语阅读素材也为老师提供了可以借鉴的教学材料。

本书分为10章，包括中国地铁历史、现状、轨道交通服务要求，地铁票务服务介绍，地铁站点介绍，地铁闸口服务介绍，地铁安全情况介绍，站台候车服务介绍，地铁突发事故介绍，地铁管理和地铁法律法规介绍，另外单设一章介绍发达国家和发展中国家地铁发展现状。附录设有地铁服务英语对照表。全书兼顾系统性和完整性，涵盖了地铁服务行业的主要内容，同时拓展了中国地铁文化和海外地铁文化的相关知识。书中用大量场景图片直观介绍乘车要领和注意事项，编排力求实用，同时也符合英语教学特点。为了方便学习，所有章节均设有操作训练，书后附有练习答案。本书内容新颖、适于操作、知识面宽、难度适中，既可以作为实用英语教材，也适合地铁服务人员自学使用。

本书由成都大学国际合作交流处杨茜和外国语学院李玲主编，杨蓓、吴虹、钟炳芳任副主编，王倩、刘颖、郭粒粒、周怡乔、杜薇、刘海、高婧、潘薇、赵雅婷、罗惠扬、李雪婷、牛晓丹参与编写。书中音频由杨蓓和美国学者David Judah Blattner朗读。本书在编写过程中得到了西南交通大学、成都地铁的大力支持，在此表示衷心感谢。

由于编者水平所限，书中难免存在疏漏之处，敬请读者批评指正。

编 者
2021年2月

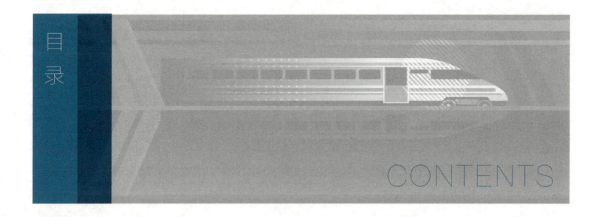

CONTENTS

Chapter One
Metro Culture — Page 001

- Unit 1 General Introduction of Chinese Metro System — 001
- Unit 2 Current Situation of China's Metro — 006
- Unit 3 Metro Service Requirements — 011

Chapter Two
Ticket Service — Page 017

- Unit 1 Introduction of Tickets — 017
- Unit 2 Selling Tickets — 022
- Unit 3 The Excess Fare — 028
- Unit 4 Ticket Policy — 032

Chapter Three
Information Signs of Metro Stations — Page 037

- Unit 1 Signs in Metro Station — 037
- Unit 2 Station Names and the Distance — 041
- Unit 3 Introduction of Facilities for the Handicapped — 047

Chapter Four
Metro Turnstile Entrance and Exit — Page 052

- Unit 1 Turnstiles and Other Facilities — 052

Unit 2	Contraband	057
Unit 3	Safety Inspection	062
Unit 4	Emergency	066

Chapter Five
Metro Safety — Page 072

| Unit 1 | Metro Exterior Safety | 072 |
| Unit 2 | Station Interior Safety | 078 |

Chapter Six
Waiting on the Platform — Page 084

| Unit 1 | Metro Schedule | 084 |
| Unit 2 | Getting On and Off the Train | 089 |

Chapter Seven
Emergency Response Guide — Page 095

Unit 1	An Earthquake in a Metro Station	095
Unit 2	A Fire in a Metro Station	098
Unit 3	An Explosion in a Metro Station	102
Unit 4	An Accident in a Metro Station	105
Unit 5	Other Situations	109

Chapter Eight
Foreign Country Metro Outlook — Page 112

| Unit 1 | The Metro System in Developed Countries | 112 |
| Unit 2 | The Metro System in Developing Countries | 120 |

Chapter Nine
Metro Service Management — Page 127

| Unit 1 | The Operations Features of Railway Transport | 127 |

Unit 2　Safety Management Modes　131
Unit 3　The Content of Metro Station Management　136

Chapter Ten
Metro Laws and Regulations　141

Unit 1　Classification of Metro Accidents　141
Unit 2　Traffic Accident Disposal　149
Unit 3　Safe Operation System　155
Unit 4　Metro Emergency Response Plan　162

附录　地铁附属设施及公共标志英语翻译一览表　169

参考文献　177

Chapter One
Metro Culture

Learning Outcomes

On completion of the module, you will be able to learn:
1. General introduction of Chinese metro system
2. Recent situation of Chinese metro
3. Main requirements of metro service

Overview of the Module

Metro is one of the low-carbon modes of transport, which can not only solve traffic jams but also release fewer pollutants. It's an ideal tool for green travel, characterized by its high-speed, convenience, large carrying capacity, punctuality, and comfort. It is the most effective mode to solve traffic problems in metropolis. Metro culture also symbolizes the civilization of a city.

Normally, China's city metro system is based on the successful experience of overseas metro, while it is designed, constructed and served according to different features of cities. Ideally, any Chinese metro system is designed for a 100-year service life. In this context where the quality and safety of metro is guaranteed, whether Chinese metro can provide quality service or not gains prominent importance. In order to improve the service level, it is urgent to understand the main requirements of metro service.

Unit 1
General Introduction of Chinese Metro System

What You Will Learn in This Unit

1. Main parts of metro system
2. History of Chinese metro system
3. Influence of metro on social development

Background

Metro is the abbreviation of métropolitain. It is an independent rail traffic system almost free from the influence of ground condition; hence, it can operate according to original design. It offers fast, safe and comfortable service to passengers. Metro is beneficial to social development with high efficiency, zero pollution and mass transport capacity. Like other rail traffic systems, metro follows practical rules in transport organization, function realization and security guarantee. In transport organization, it must obey centralized control, unified command and be operated by train working diagram. In function realization, all relative departments should be kept in good condition, such as tunnels, routes, power supply, metro vehicles, communication, signals, electromechanical devices of stations and fire protection system. In security guarantee, it keeps running intervals and right routes by effective train operation and devices in good condition. All must be regulated by metro principles and rules. In general, metro is a complicated system involving cooperation of multiple departments and drive safety in scheduled time.

Part I Getting Started

1. The following are the pictures of railway system. Write down the English expressions below.

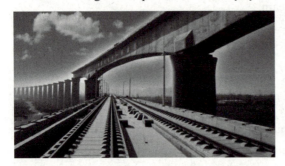
（1）_____

（2）_____

（3）_____

（4）_____

2. Work in pairs and list other parts of a metro system, and give a brief introduction of their functions.

Part II Studying

A. Conversations

Conversation 1

M1-1

Linda just came to Beijing to be a teacher. She is interested in Chinese culture and history, so she asks one of the station staff members(SM) about the Beijing metro.

SM: Hello! Can I help you?

Linda: Yes. I'm new here. It's my first time to take the Beijing metro. Can you tell me something about it?

SM: Of course.

Linda: What's the length of the Beijing metro and how many lines are there in total?

SM: It's 350 kilometers and there are 16 lines covering all the areas of Beijing.

Linda: When did it begin to be built?

SM: It is the earliest metro in China. It's been in service since 1965. Now it's the longest metro in China.

Linda: Do you have a metro map? I want to take it home to study, because I'm living in Beijing University now. Maybe the metro is the most convenient way for me.

SM: No problem. Wait a minute. I will bring one to you.

(One minute later.)

SM: Here you are.

Linda: Thank you so much. By the way, can you tell me some information about the ticket?

SM: Yes, madam. The ticket depends on the distance. The starting price is 3 yuan per person within 6 kilometers. From 6 to 12 kilometers, you will be charged 4 yuan, and after 12 kilometers, one more yuan will be added for each 10 kilometers. There's no limit.

Linda: Oh, it's reasonable. Thank you very much. Bye-bye.

SM: If you have any questions, you can ask any staff member. Welcome to China. Bye-bye.

Conversation 2

Linda discussed the Sydney and Beijing metro systems with her new classmate Li Jia, a Chinese girl.

Linda: Li Jia, I went to the railway station today and had a great feeling about the Beijing metro.

M1-2

Li Jia: Yeah. There's a big change in the Beijing metro. It's our favourite transport. It's very convenient.

Linda: In my hometown Sydney, the metro connects with the railway. We can use the Opal Card to take the metro, train, and even the ferry.

Li Jia: In Beijing, we have the transportation card. It can be applied on the bus and in the metro, but It can't be used for trains. You know China is a country with a complex train network. It's really hard to cover all in only one card.

Linda: When is the earliest train in Beijing?

Li Jia: It begins around 5 AM and ends at around 11 PM, but there's a little difference among stations. You'd better ask the station staff.

Linda: It's nice. I often worry about how to get back. In that case, I can take the metro.

B. Words & Expressions

staff /stɑːf/ *n.* 职员，工作人员
length /leŋθ/ *n.* 长度；全长
cover /ˈkʌvə/ *v.* 覆盖
metro /ˈmetrəʊ/ *n.* 地道，地铁
convenient /kənˈviːniənt/ *adj.* 方便的，合宜的

charge /tʃɑːdʒ/ *v.* 索价；对……索费
reasonable /ˈriːznəbl/ *adj.* 合理的，适当的，明理的
railway /ˈreilwei/ *n.* 铁路；铁路系统；铁道；铁路公司

M1-3

transport /træn'spɔ:t/ *n.* 运输；交通运输系统
apply /ə'plaɪ/ *v.* 应用；实施；适用
metro system 地铁系统
connect with 与……连接
depend on 依靠；与……相关
starting price 起价

C. Notes

1. metro 和 subway 的区别：subway 在美国是"地铁"，在英国是"地下人行通道"；美国人称"地下人行通道"为 pedestrian crossing。英国的地铁是 tube，metro 或 underground railway，法语国家也是 metro，但是 subway 在法国是"地下行人通道"的意思。

2. the earliest metro in China：北京地铁始建于1965年7月1日，1969年10月1日第一条地铁线路建成通车，使北京成为中国第一个拥有地铁的城市。北京地铁一期工程全长23.6千米，设17座车站和1座车辆段。

3. metro system：地铁系统主要由地铁路网、地铁车辆、地铁信号、地铁通信、地铁供电、地铁环境控制与车站设备、地铁运输组织及各控制系统组成。

Part III Your Turn

A. Speaking Practice

Give a general report about the following history of China metro development in English. You can use the words and expressions below.

19世纪是桥的世纪，20世纪是高层建筑的世纪，21世纪为了节约能源、保护环境，人类必须大量利用地下空间。因此，21世纪对人类来说是地下空间的世纪。1965年，北京地铁成为中国最早的地铁线路。目前，北京地铁日客运量1000万人次左右，大大缓解了首都的交通压力。天津地铁是中国第二条地铁，已建地铁线路6条，日客运量达100万人次左右。中国第三个修建地铁的城市是上海，始建于1990年初，现已建18条地铁线路，日均客运量达1000万人次左右。另外，广州、深圳、南京等城市均已建成各自的城市地铁网。在建城市还有西安、成都、哈尔滨、杭州、沈阳、长沙等。地铁的修建大大缓解了城市交通拥挤的现象，促进了城市的健康发展。

tall building   save energy   protect environment   underground relieves   traffic pressure
daily passenger   transportation volume   metro network   healthy development

B. Reading Practice

Read the passage and answer the questions below.

China is a **relative** newcomer to build metros in its major cities, and there was even a ban on new projects in 2002. However, this policy was **reversed** in 2004 because there has been an explosion in metro construction. As Hans-Ulrich Riedel reports, 39 cities in China have metros totalling 6,600 km.

China only opened its first metro line in 1969 in the capital Beijing, although foreigners were **initially** forbidden to use it. There was then an 11-year gap until the country's second metro line was completed when Tianjin opened its first line in 1980. Up to this time, the bicycle was by far the most common form of transport in Chinese cities.

Once economic **liberalisation** got underway in the 1980s, two more cities began to plan metros starting with Shanghai, which opened its first 6.6km section in May 1993, followed by Guangzhou with a 5km line in June 1997. While Beijing, Shanghai and Guangzhou set about developing large metro networks during the 1990s, other cities began to plan metros but without **approval** of the state which was probably **daunt**ed by the scale of investment that would require. In an attempt to stop cities planning new metro projects, the government issued an **edict** in October 2002 banning their construction except for **schemes** already underway. Nevertheless, some cities continued to work behind the scenes on their metro plans.

The ban didn't last long as the need to address the explosive growth of China's cities, increasing **motorisation** which rapidly killed off the use of bicycles in urban areas, and worsening pollution forced a **fundamental** rethink by the government which lifted the ban in 2004. Metro construction received further **impetus** with the awarding of the 2008 Summer Olympic Games to Beijing and World Expo 2010 to Shanghai.

Since then, vast sums have been invested in metro projects allowing Chinese cities to leapfrog ahead of their global **counterparts**. Beijing with a 16-line 637km metro and Shanghai with a 772km system of 19 lines now have by far the largest networks in the world **usurping** cities like New York (394km), Mexico City (226km), London (430km), Paris (215km), Madrid (284km), Moscow (425km), Seoul (327km) and Tokyo (304km). Even Guangzhou, with its 240.8km eight-line metro, now ranks among the world's top 11 systems.

The scale of construction in China is quite breathtaking and in another league compared with metro construction in other parts of the world. Most cities tend to build one line at a time or short **extensions** to existing lines due to the high cost of constructing metro lines in densely-populated urban areas and the engineering resources required. Not so in China where a **staggering** 1349km of new lines was brought into operation. A further 1600km of new lines will open. The biggest of these projects is in Nanjing, where three new lines totalling 51km were due to open, although following an accident during construction, the opening of Line 3 has been postponed until 2015. Beijing is opening fourteen extensions which will add 134.95km to its network, Wuxi opened its first 29.4km line in July, 2014 and **inaugurates** a fourth line next month, while Chongqing will complete seven extensions totalling 123.1km and Shanghai two totalling 80.81km.

Shenzhen, China's first and most successful special economic zone, which was established to the north of Hong Kong, illustrates the scale of development. Shenzhen has grown from a small fishing village when the SEZ(Special Economic Zone) was established in 1979 to a metropolis of over 10 million inhabitants, far outstripping its much older southern neighbour which has a population of 7.2 million. Shenzhen currently has an eight-line metro totalling 304km but it is building another eight lines. In 2020, Shenzhen invested 10.8 billion RMB in metro construction. In addition, construction of a separate light rail system has completed in the northern district of Longhua.

Metro projects must be submitted to the National Development and Reform Commission for approval, and the number of projects receiving approval has increased dramatically since the Beijing Olympics in 2008.

Words & Expressions

relative / 'relətɪv/ *adj.* 相对的
reverse /rɪ'vəs/ *v.* 翻转
initially / ɪ'nɪʃəli/ *adv.* 最初地
liberalisation /ˌlɪbərəlaɪ'zeɪʃən/ *n.* 开放
approval /ə'pruːvl/ *n.* 同意
daunt /dɔːnt/ *v.* 使气馁
edict /'iːdɪkt/ *n.* 法令
scheme /skɪːm/ *n.* 方案，计划
motorisation /məʊtəri'zeɪʃn/ *n.* 动力化

fundamental /ˌfʌndə'mentl/ *adj.* 基本的
impetus / 'ɪmpɪtəs/ *n.* 动力
counterpart /'kaʊntəpɑːt/ *n.* 相对应的人或物
usurp /juː'zɜːp/ *v.* 篡夺、超越
extension /ɪk'stenʃn/ *n.* 延伸
staggering /'stægərɪŋ/ *adj.* 令人震惊的
inaugurate /ɪ'nɔːgjəreɪt/ *v.* 开辟

M1-4

Questions

1. What is the second metro line in China?
2. Why would China continue building metro even though the government banned it some time?
3. Which metro is the longest in the world? What's its length?
4. Can a city build its metro alone without any permission?
5. Do a study of your city metro line and know the time of its construction and the length.

Unit 2
Current Situation of China's Metro

What You Will Learn in This Unit

1. City network
2. Metro development
3. Some problems of metro development

Part I Getting Started

1. Do you know the names of the following metro logos? Try to write the city names on the underlines.

_____   _____   _____

2. Can you list other 5 logos? Draw them and write down their names below.

Part II Studying

A. Conversations

Conversation 1

Jim is from London. He is amazed by the Beijing Metro service because he thought China's metro service must be inferior to that of London. Liu Hang is talking with him about the current metro system in China.

M1-5

Jim: Liu Hang. I couldn't believe my eyes when I took the metro today.

Liu Hang: What's wrong?

Jim: It's unbelievable that your metro is as convenient as London's. You know London has the oldest metro system in the world. The metro network spreads over all the streets and districts of London. We don't need to take a car for work or school. However, I experienced the convenience of Beijing's metro. It's also great.

Liu Hang: Yes. The Beijing Metro is the oldest one in China. Now it has 16 lines and covers 11 districts of Beijing. More than 300 stations have been built. The total distance is more than 700 kilometers. I believe it's longer than that of London.

Jim: Yes, exactly. It's really amazing. Could you tell me the population of Beijing? It may be related to the distance of metro development.

Liu Hang: If I tell you, you wouldn't believe it. It's around 20 million.

Jim: Oh, my God. It's a shocking number. It must be the largest city in the world.

Liu Hang: Maybe. You know China really has a big population.

Jim: So it built the longest metro in the world.

Liu Hang: I think so.

Conversation 2

Richard was discussing with He Jia about the Shanghai Metro and the New York Metro.

Richard: I really love living in Shanghai. The weather is pleasant and the local people are really friendly.

He Jia: Thank you. Shanghai is one of the biggest cities in China. It developed so fast in recent years.

Richard: Yes. More and more skyscrapers are being built. However, the Shanghai Metro is not very satisfying, even though there are 19 lines. I still feel nervous about taking it, especially during rush hours.

He Jia: Why?

Richard: It's always crowded. I'm wondering when it was built and why its design couldn't meet the needs of local people.

He Jia: It's said that the Shanghai Metro was built in 1995.

Richard: The New York Metro has a longer history. It was built in 1904, but it still works well. It can transport 5 million people daily. At present, you can still see and experience the over 100-year-old magic engineering project.

He Jia: It's true. However, did you know the Shanghai Metro is the third largest metro system in the world? The population in Shanghai is around 20 million.

Richard: That's true. I really hope it'll become better to satisfy the commuters and the tourists.

He Jia: I believe so.

B. Words & Expressions

network /ˈnetwɜːk/ n. 网状系统
convenience /kənˈviːniəns/ n. 方便，便利的事物
shocking /ˈʃɒkɪŋ/ adj. 可怕的，过分的
skyscraper /ˈskaɪskreɪpə(r)/ n. 摩天大楼，超高层大楼；特别高的东西
erect /ɪˈrekt/ v. 使竖立，树立，使直立

satisfying /ˈsætɪsfaɪɪŋ/ adj. 令人满足的；令人满意的
design /dɪˈzaɪn/ n. 设计；花样；图案
commuter /kəˈmjuːtə(r)/ n. 通勤者；经常往返者

C. Notes

1. Shanghai Metro：上海轨道交通，又称上海地铁，其第一条线路——上海轨道交通1号线于1993年5月28日开通试运营，是继北京地铁、天津地铁建成通车后中国内地（大陆）投入运营的第三个城市轨道交通系统。上海轨道交通由上海申通地铁集团有限公司负责运营，按照上海市物价主管部门批复的轨道交通网络票价体系计价，有多种票价优惠政策和车票种类。

截至2021年1月，上海轨道交通共开通线路19条，全网运营线路总长772千米。

2. New York Metro：纽约地铁是美国纽约市的城市轨道交通系统，是全球历史最悠久的公共地下铁路系统之一，也是国际地铁联盟（COMET）的成员。纽约地铁拥有468座车站，商业营运路线长度为245英里（394千米），用以营运的轨道长度约为665英里（约1,070千米），总铺轨长度达850英里（约1,370千米）。其名虽为地铁，但约40%的路轨形式为地面或高架。纽约地铁是世界上最著名的十大地铁之一。

3. Chinese metro problems：地铁造价高达每千米数亿元，而且建成后每年需要相当大的资金投入运营，投入大、收效慢，巨大的资金压力对地方财政是巨大的负担。特别是我国二三

线城市，地方财政本来就比较紧张，再用有限的资金投入到地铁建设中，严重拖累了地方经济发展。同时，地铁修建带来1~3年地铁沿线居民生活不便，也严重影响沿街的商业体。另外，地铁在设计上还未做到100年的规划。很多线路老旧无法重新修建，为将来安全运行带来了极大的隐患。

Part III Your Turn

A. Speaking Practice

Translate the following Chinese into English.

1. 上海地铁：上海地铁，其第一条线路——上海轨道交通1号线是继北京地铁、天津地铁建成通车后中国大陆（内地）投入运营的第三个城市轨道交通系统。截至2021年，上海轨道交通共开通线路19条，全网运营总里程达772千米，在世界城市地铁长度排名当中高居榜首，是世界上线路最长的地铁。

2. 北京地铁：规划始于1953年，工程始建于1965年，最早的线路竣工于1969年，是中国第一个地铁系统。2017年，北京地铁年客运量突破45亿人次，居全球第一，日均客流量过千万已成常态。

3. 长春地铁：长春是中国第一个有地铁规划的城市。

4. 香港地铁：是全球独一无二最具商业价值的地铁，经济效益十分可观。香港地铁每日乘客量超过245万人次，成为世界上最繁忙的铁路系统之一。

5. 天津地铁：天津地铁1号线最浅处埋深仅2米，是世界上埋深最浅的地铁。

6. 重庆地铁：重庆轨道交通6号线，有一座埋深超过60米、深度居全国地铁站第一的车站——红土地站。车站内电扶梯的提升高度达到60米，甚至大大超过重庆人引以为傲的两路口皇冠大扶梯。

B. Reading Practice

Read the following passage and make a judgment of the exercises. Write T for True and F for False.

Beijing and Other Key Cities Plan for 10-fold Expansion of Metro Railways

The mainland China is planning to have 11,700km of metro railway by 2050 to keep up with the new leaders' ambitions to speed up urbanization. Mainland cities will expand their metro railways almost tenfold by 2050 to keep up with the aggressive **urbanisation** drive.

By 2050, mainland cities will have 11,700 kilometres of metro railway, **accounting for** at least half the world's metro railway, said a **bond prospectus** of China CNR Corporation, a leading **rolling stock manufacturer**. This is nearly 10 times the 1,688 kilometres of operating metro railway in 14 cities at the end of 2011.

By 2019, there were 6,730 kilometres of metro railway, said the Shanghai-listed firm's prospectus. In the next few years, 1.6 trillion yuan (HK$2 trillion) would be invested in metro rail construction, CNR said.

"Our nation's urban railway has entered a new stage of development. China has already become the world's biggest metro railway market," it said.

Incoming Premier Li Keqiang had put a lot of emphasis on urbanisation, said Karen Li, JP

Morgan Analyst. "Absolutely, metro building is linked to urbanisation," she said.

In November, Li Keqiang wrote in an article in *People's Daily* that urbanisation was "a huge engine" of the mainland's future economic growth.

Once the nation's new leadership takes over next month, more metro projects would be approved, said Karen Li. "More metro projects will begin construction this year." Companies working on mainland metro rail projects all said "there would be heavy metro investment".

Tier-one cities such as Beijing are **congested** and polluted, and so they need more metro railways to alleviate these problems, Karen Li explained.

The state-owned firm invested 492.6 billion yuan in 2019, and 470.9 billion yuan in 2020. The investment will go into metro rail equipment, **electro-mechanical** systems, technology, logistics, financial services, as well as non-rail industries such as new energy and green cars.

CNR and CSR Corporation, a Shanghai and Hong Kong-listed firm, produces nearly all the mainland's rolling stock.

CNR plans to issue 4 billion yuan of one-year bonds, which will be used to repay bank loans. Its short-term debt nearly tripled from 12.2 billion yuan at the end of 2010 to 33.89 billion yuan on September 30 last year, while its accounts **receivable** tripled from 10.27 billion yuan to 30.54 billion yuan over this period. In the first nine months of last year, CNR suffered a net operating cash outflow of 5.48 billion yuan. The company's **gearing ratio** stood at 69.25 per cent till September 30 last year.

"The company's short-term debt has grown rapidly, its **liquidity** pressure has increased," said Chengxin. In the first nine months of last year, CNR's revenue increased 0.2 per cent to 64.3 billion yuan, while net profit grew 9.1 per cent to 2.34 billion yuan.

Words & Expressions

urbanization /ˌɜːbənaɪˈzeɪʃn/ *n.* 都市化；文雅化
account for 说明；对……负有责任；（在数量方面）占
bond /bɒnd/ *n.* 结合，契约，债券
prospectus /prəˈspektəs/ *n.* 计划书，招投书
rolling stock manufacturer 机车车辆制造厂

congest /kənˈdʒest/ *v.* 拥挤；充满
electro-mechanical 电机的
receivable /rɪˈsiːvəbl/ *adj.* 可接受的；可承认的
gearing ratio 资产负债比率
liquidity /lɪˈkwɪdəti/ *n.* 流动性；流畅

M1-8

After reading, write T for True and F for False.

(   ) 1. By 2015, mainland cities will have 11,700 kilometres of metro railway, accounting for at least half the world's metro railway.

(   ) 2. Incoming Premier Li Keqiang had put a lot of emphasis on urbanization, and metro building is linked to urbanization. In this way, metro building is a necessity.

(   ) 3. China's railway can make a lot of profit.

(   ) 4. China has already become the world's biggest metro railway market.

(   ) 5. The state-owned firm always invests 10 billion yuan in metro building.

Unit 3
Metro Service Requirements

What You Will Learn in This Unit

1. Standardization of facilities
2. Standardization of personal service
3. Standardization of management

Part I Getting Started

Do you know the English names and Chinese names of the following facilities?

(1) _____

(2) _____

(3) _____

(4) _____

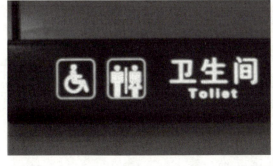

(5) _____

(6) _____

(7) _____ (8) _____

Part II Studying

A. Conversation

Liu Li has worked in a metro station for 5 years. Now she is training the new staff on service standards.

M1-9

Liu Li: When you talk with a foreigner, you should address him or her as madam or sir, and ask "What can I do for you?" "May I help you?" or "Can I help you?"

(The staff follow her to practice.)

Liu Li: When you want foreign passengers to wait for you, you should say "Wait a moment, please." or "Can you wait a minute? I will come back soon."

(The staff follow her to practice.)

Liu Li: When you find that a foreigner breaks the regulations or law, you should go towards him or her and tell the reason. The beginning sentence should be like this, "Sorry, sir, it's forbidden to smoke here." "Excuse me, madam, your baby shouldn't pee here. There's a toilet."

Liu Li: When you find that a foreigner doesn't know how to buy a ticket from a vending machine, you can approach him or her and show the instructions on the machine and direct him or her to buy it. Use the words like this, "Sir or Madam, first you will see notice the machine accepts 5-yuan, 10-yuan and 50-yuan bills and coins. Find the destination on the electric map and press it, and then it will show the bill. After that, put your money in the slot. The machine will calculate the change and then offer you the ticket and the change in the box."

Liu Li: If the foreign passenger wants a receipt, you can ask him or her to get one in the ticket office. Are you clear?

(The staff begin to practice.)

Liu Li: When the passenger wants to take the escalator, you should warn him or her like this, "Please stand on the right and hold the handrail. Please mind the steps."

(The staff follow her to practice.)

Liu Li: When the passengers are waiting for the train, you should inform them like this, "Please wait in line and mind the gap between the train and the platform."

After the class, the new staff realize that any job needs full preparation and a good attitude.

B. Words & Expressions

address /əˈdres/ v. 向……说话；称呼
forbidden /fəˈbɪdn/ adj. 被禁止的，禁止的
pee /piː/ n. & v. 撒尿（俚语）
approach /əˈprəʊtʃ/ v. 靠近，接近；动手处理
instruction /ɪnˈstrʌkʃn/ n. 指示；教导；用法说明
direct /dɪˈrekt/ v. 指示，命令，指挥；指导
accept /əkˈsept/ v. 领受，接受，认可；相信
destination /ˌdestɪˈneɪʃn/ n. 目的地
slot /slɒt/ n. 狭长孔；投币口；狭缝，缝隙
calculate /ˈkælkjuleɪt/ v. 计算；预测
change /tʃeɪndʒ/ n. 找回的零钱
receipt /rɪˈsiːt/ n. 收据；收入
escalator /ˈeskəleɪtə(r)/ n. 电动扶梯

warn /wɔːn/ v. 警告，注意；发出警告
handrail /ˈhændreɪl/ n. 栏杆；扶手
inform /ɪnˈfɔːm/ v. 通知，通告
gap /ɡæp/ n. 缝隙；间断；分歧
platform /ˈplætfɔːm/ n. 月台，坛；讲台
realize /ˈrɪəlaɪz/ v. 领悟，认识到，了解
attitude /ˈætɪtjuːd/ n. 态度；看法；姿势
break the regulations or law 犯规或犯法
vending machine 售票机
electric map 电子地图

M1-10

C. Notes

地铁站常规服务规范

1. 站外疏导

- 请您听从工作人员的指挥，顺序进站。Follow the order, please.
- 请您不要拥挤，顺序进站。Don't push. Please keep order.
- 目前地铁客流较大，我们正在采取限流措施，请您配合。Now the station is full of crowded passengers. We are taking measures to limit. Thank you for your cooperation.

2. 安全检查

正常疏导

- 您好。Hello.
- 谢谢合作。Thank you for your cooperation.
- 乘客您好，请您顺序安检，谢谢合作。Dear passenger, please keep order for checking. Thank you for your cooperation.
- 为保证乘车安全，请您自觉接受安检，谢谢合作。In order to keep passengers' safety, you are required to be checked. Thank you for your cooperation.

拒检情况时

- 您好，为保证乘车安全，请您接受安检，谢谢配合。Hello, in order to keep passengers' safety, you are required to be checked. Thank you for your cooperation.
- 您好，根据《×××城市交通安全运营管理办法》规定，请您接受、配合安检。Hello, you are required to be checked according to our regulation. Thank you for your cooperation.
- 依据×××市第×××号令，请您接受安检。According to the government requirement, you need a check.

发现可疑物时

- 您好，您的箱包（挎包、箱子、行李等）需要进行开包检查，请您打开箱包，谢谢合作。Hello, your suitcase (handbag, case, luggage, etc.) should be opened for checking. Please open it. Thank you for your cooperation.

遇乘客携带禁、限带品时

- 您好，您携带的物品属于轨道交通运营企业公示的禁、限带品，不能携带该物品乘坐地铁。Your belongings are forbidden for the metro. You can't take them into the metro.
- 请您换乘其他交通工具，谢谢合作。You should change to another transportation tool. Thank you for your cooperation.

乘客寻求帮助无法解答时

- 对不起，我正在执勤，无法离岗，请您询问其他工作人员。Sorry, I'm on duty. Please ask other staff.

3. 解答线路询问

- 您好，您先要乘坐去往×××方向的列车，到×××站下车后，换乘×××线，再乘坐去往×××方向的列车，到×××站下车，就可以了。Hello, you should take the train to…, and get off in…station and transfer Line…. Take the train to…and get off at…station.
- 你要去×××处，应从×××出口出。If you will go to…, you should go to Exit ×××.

4. 人工售票

售票服务过程

- 您好。Hello.
- 请您稍等。Please wait for a moment.
- 请您按顺序排队购票。Please wait in line to buy the ticket.
- 您好，请问您买几张票？Hello, how many tickets do you want to buy?
- 收您×××元。/您的钱正好。It's…
- 找您×××元。请收好。Here's your money.

售卡充值过程

- 您好，请问您充值多少元？Hello, how much do you want to recharge?
- 您充值×××元，请您确认（说话过程中，用手指向客显屏）。Here is your account.
- 找您×××元，请收好。（将卡、找零、水单、发票同时交于乘客。）Here's your change.

收款、找零规范

- 请您换一张。谢谢。（当乘客手持残币、假币时说。）Please change another one. Thank you.

有乘客等候不耐烦，应该进行安抚

- 对不起，让您久等了。Sorry, so long for your waiting.

5. 监票进/出站

- 请您右手持卡，有序刷卡。Hold the card in your right hand and swipe the card in order.
- 带小孩的乘客请让小孩先行。Let the children go ahead.
- 车票回收，请您投票出站。Put your card into the slot and exit.
- 请您刷卡（投票），快速进/出站。Please swipe the card and move on.

6. 候车组织和乘降组织

候车组织

- 请您站在黄色安全线以内候车。Please wait in the yellow line.
- 请您不要倚靠屏蔽门，以免发生危险。Please keep clear from the door.
- 车站候车乘客较多，请您分散上车。The platform is crowded, please keep order.

- 请您分散候车，谢谢合作。Please scatter to wait for the train. Thank you for your cooperation.

乘降组织
- 现在是乘车高峰时段，请您分散车门上车。It's the rush hour. Please get on the train in another queue.
- 列车即将进站，请您注意安全，往后站。The train is arriving. Please take care and step back.
- 请您让开车门、先下后上，上不去的乘客请您等候下次列车，谢谢合作。Please keep clear from the door and let the passengers aboard get off first. Please wait for the next train. Thank you for your cooperation.
- 请您抓紧时间，先下后上，快速乘降。Please hurry up. Let the passengers abroad get off the train first.
- 请您往车厢中部走。Please move towards the middle of the train.
- 车门即将关闭，请等候下次列车。The door is closing. Please wait for the next train.
- 请不要抢上抢下，顺序上下。Please keep in line.
- 请不要冲撞屏蔽门，耐心等待下次列车。Please keep clear from the door and wait for the next train.

7. **乘梯组织**
- 请您文明乘梯。Please keep order.
- 请您扶好扶手。Please hold the handrail.
- 请您靠右站立、左侧通行。Please stand on the right, and pass on the left.
- 请照顾好老人及儿童。Please take care of the old and the children.

Part III Your Turn

A. Speaking Practice

Read the following sentences, and understand the meanings.

1. The train is arriving. Please mind the gap between the train and the platform. This train stops service at ... station.
2. Please take care of your children and belongings. Thank you!
3. Please be ready to exit as the platform is very busy.
4. For your safety, please stand back from the platform screen doors.
5. Please move along the platform to the middle of the train for easier boarding.
6. When you use the escalators, stand still, hold the handrail. Please don't run or walk in the wrong direction.
7. To keep a clean and healthy environment, please don't smoke or litter in trains or stations. Please offer your seats to anyone in need. Thank you for your cooperation.
8. Welcome to ... station, we hope you will have a pleasant journey.

B. Reading Practice

Customer Amenities

Passenger **amenities** are those elements provided at a **transit** stop, transit center, and station stops to **enhance** comfort, convenience, and security. The metro will provide customers with **applicable** amenities and available resources. In some instances, the metro will partner with

municipalities to provide the appropriate amenities. Amenities include such items as shelters, benches, vending machines, **trash receptacles**, lighting, restrooms and telephones.

<u>Benches</u> provide comfort for waiting passengers, help identify the stop or station, and are a more affordable **alternative** than shelters.

<u>Elevator/Escalators</u> provide **accessibility** for those who otherwise cannot use stairs to elevated station stops.

<u>Lighting</u> increases visibility, increases perceptions of comfort and security, and discourages misuse of bus stops once transit operations are no longer in service.

<u>Public Restrooms</u> may be provided at transit centers and maintained for public safety and convenience.

<u>Shelters</u> provide comfort for waiting passengers, protection from climate conditions and help identify the stop or station.

<u>Telephones/Intercoms</u> provide **access to** transit information and emergencies.

<u>Trash receptacles</u> provide a place to discard trash and keep bus stops and surroundings clean.

<u>Vending machines</u> can provide newspapers and snacks to passengers while waiting for a transit vehicle.

When transit service is not provided near one's home, driving to a park-and-ride lot or riding a bicycle to transit may be **viable** alternatives. Park and ride lots are especially important amenity for transit riders.

Words & Expressions

amenity /əˈmiːnəti/ *n.* 文化设施，便利设施
transit /ˈtrænsɪt/ *n.* 运输，运送；中转
enhance /ɪnˈhɑːns/ *v.* 提高，增强，增进
applicable /ˈæplɪkəbl/ *adj.* 可应用的；可适用的
municipality /mjuːˌnɪsɪˈpæləti/ *n.* 自治市；市政当局
trash receptacles 垃圾桶

alternative /ɔːlˈtɜːnətɪv/ *n.* 选择，二者择一
accessibility /əkˌsesəˈbɪləti/ *n.* 易接近，可亲；可以得到
access to 接近；使用……的机会
viable /ˈvaɪəbl/ *adj.* 可实施的，切实可行的

M1-11

Can you find the corresponding words to the following Chinese terms?

照明装置 _____   电话或对讲机 _____
等候区 _____   售票机 _____
公共休息室 _____   电动扶梯 _____
长凳休息区 _____   便利设施 _____
垃圾箱 _____

Chapter Two
Ticket Service

Learning Outcomes

On completion of the module, you will be able to:
1. Provide passengers with ticket information
2. Show guests the process to buy tickets
3. Solve the problem of excess fare
4. Explain ticket principles to passengers

Overview of the Module

　　The ticket system is the main part of metro system. The traditional ticket selling is conducted manually, which shows inefficiency and waste of human resources. It's difficult to face the large number of passengers in rush hours. The application of the computerized auto system can greatly improve the metro operation efficiency, save human resources and enhance management.

　　Although the ticket system is well-improved, different problems still appear in the selling process, such as the loss of tickets, expired tickets, free passes, overtime rides, receipts, etc. They all need qualified staff to explain and solve.

　　In this case, the chapter will help the metro staff members to better understand the ticket policy and grasp the skill of helping foreign passengers buy tickets and explaining relative ticket principles to them.

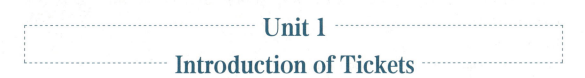

Unit 1
Introduction of Tickets

What You Will Learn in This Unit

1. One way tickets
2. Round-trip tickets
3. Rechargeable card and commute card

Part I Getting Started

1. The following are the different tickets. Write their correct names below.

This is _____

This is _____

This is _____

This is _____

2. Can you find other kinds of tickets? List some and discuss with your partner which one is the most convenient.

Part II Studying

A. Conversations

Conversation 1

Steven and his family have arrived at Shanghai Hongqiao Airport. They are now planning to get to Nanjing Road. Jenny, Steven's sister studying at Shanghai University, is waiting for them at Nanjing Road. Steven wants to buy some tickets from the ticket machine but he doesn't know how to do it.

M2-1

Steven : Excuse me.

SM : Yes. Welcome to the Shanghai Metro. How can I help you?

Seven: I want to buy tickets from the machine. Can you show me how to do it?

SM: Which station do you want to go, sir?

Steven: I'd like to get to Nanjing Road.

SM: Okay. Let me show you. First, choose Line 2 and then press the button of Nanjing Road Station as your destination. Then, choose how many tickets you're going to buy. The machine accepts 20-

yuan, 10-yuan and 5-yuan notes as well as one yuan coins. It's five yuan per person from this station (Hongqiao Airport) to Nanjing Road.

Steven: Thanks.

Steven is seeking some money from his wallet but then realizes that he only has one hundred notes. And then he goes back to ask the metro staff.

Steven: Hi, again. I don't have a smaller bill. Where can I break a hundred?

SM: You can go to the ticket center. This way, please. (Using her hand to direct Steven to the ticket center.)

Steven: Thanks, again!

Steven is at the ticket center now.

Steven: Hi, I want two tickets to Nanjing Road but I don't have any small change.

SM: OK, let me get you some change then.

SM: Have a nice day.

Steven: Thank you.

Conversation 2

Steven at last met Jenny at Nanjing Road Station.

Steven : Jenny! So happy to see you!

Jenny: Me, too! How's the metro? Find any problems riding it?

Steven: Not at all. I bought the tickets at the machine. The staff were really nice. They helped me a lot, actually.

Jenny: Since you and Mother will go out and about, you might want to buy a Shanghai Public Transportation Card so that you don't have to buy tickets each time as you take the metro. It's quite convenient.

Steven: Wonderful!

Jenny: Yep. Especially now that there's a lot of road maintenance going on, traffic gets quite bad especially during rush hours. And to make it more convenient for people here, they give you 10% off on the tickets after spending over 70 yuan. Besides, if you transfer from one bus or metro, one yuan can be saved. It's a bargain.

Steven: Fantastic. Let's go and get one.

Jenny shows Steven and Mother to a ticket center.

Steven: Hi, we want to buy two Public Transportation Cards, please.

SM: Okay. How much would you like to put in each card? There will be a 20-yuan deposit for each card as well. You will get this money back when you return the card. The card expires one year after purchase. You may recharge your card at ticket centers, some banks, ticket machines, or some convenience stores. There's no limit to the recharged amount.

Steven: Okay. We'll get 50 yuan on each card.

SM: Okay. Here are your cards.

Steven: Thanks. May I have a receipt as well?

SM: No problem. Here you are.

Steven: Thanks a lot.

B. Words & Expressions

choose /tʃuːz/ *v.* 选择；挑选
note /nəʊt/ *n.* 纸币
bill /bɪl/ *n.* 账单；清单；钞票
public /ˈpʌblɪk/ *n.* 公众，民众
transfer /trænsˈfɜː(r)/ *v.* 转移，换车
bargain /ˈbɑːɡən/ *n.* 特价商品，便宜货；买卖，交易；廉价
fantastic /ˌfænˈtæstɪk/ *adj.* 奇妙的，空想的，稀奇的
deposit /dɪˈpɒzɪt/ *n.* 存款，堆积物，定金，押金
expire /ɪkˈspaɪə(r)/ *v.* 期满；到期
purchase /ˈpɜːtʃəs/ *v.* 买，购买

limit /ˈlɪmɪt/ *n.* 限制；限度
Line 2 二号线
press the button 按按钮
ticket center 票务中心/售票处
break a hundred 100元找零
transportation card 交通卡
ticket machine 售票机
road maintenance 道路维护
rush hour 高峰期
give you 10% off 降价10%
convenience store 便利店
recharged amount 充值额度

M2-3

C. Notes

1.自动售票机可接受5元、10元纸币和1元硬币。
The ticket machines only accept 5 yuan notes, 10 yuan notes and 1 yuan coins.

2.自动售票机可以充值天府通卡。
You may recharge your Tianfu Card at the ticket machine.

3.您好，请选择你的目的站。
Hello, please choose your destination station.

4.请选择你购买的张数。
Please select the number of tickets/how many tickets you're buying.

5.请从取票口取走您的车票。
Please collect your ticket (and change) at the tray in the bottom.

6.不好意思，本机零钱不足，请到其他机器购票。
I'm sorry. This ticket machine is out of change. Please use another one.

7.请到这边办理退票业务。
Please come here to return your ticket.

Part III Your Turn

A. Speaking Practice

1. Take one of the roles according to the prompts given below in Chinese.

Situation: It's afternoon and a foreign guest comes to you to ask the information about the ticket.

Guest	Staff
咨询对方从这个地方到市中心怎么买票	询问对方具体是市中心的什么地方，并告诉他本市的卡片类型和购票方式
询问对方充值卡详情	告诉他充值卡的类型和相关政策

Guest	Staff
询问到机场的地铁情况	告诉他到机场的成人票、儿童票以及往返票的优惠政策

2. Discussion

Work in groups and discuss the following topics.

(1) As a metro staff, how can you become a qualified one?

(2) Do you agree that all guests should buy tickets from the ticket machine? Why or why not?

B. Reading Practice

On Oyster

You can put money on your Oyster card and then use it as Pay As You **Go credit** to pay for journeys on bus, Tube, **tram**, **DLR**, London **Overground**, **TFL Rail** and most National Rail services within London. You can also use it to pay discounted fares on the Emirates Air Line and some river services.

Pay As You Go fares are generally cheaper than paying cash. Oyster works out the cheapest fare for all your journeys in one day so you'll never pay more than the daily cap.

Pay As You Go credit on your Oyster card never expires——it stays there until you use it. Once you've used up your credit, simply **top it up** to use again. If you don't use up all of your Pay As You Go credit you may be able to get it **refunded** at a Tube station ticket machine or a Travel Information Centre.

How to use Pay As You Go

On Tube, DLR, London Overground, TFL Rail and most National Rail services in London:

• Touch your Oyster card on a yellow card reader to start a journey. A Pay As You Go fare will be **deducted**.

• At the end of your journey, touch your Oyster card out on the yellow card reader ——doing this means you'll be charged the correct pay as you go fare for the route you've taken.

If you don't touch in or out, you might be charged a **maximum pay** as you go fare and risk a penalty fare.

On bus and tram services

Just touch your Oyster card on the yellow card reader at the start of your journey. You don't need to touch out when you get off.

Peak and off-peak

Different fares apply depending on which services you use and when. If you're using Oyster Pay As You Go, you can get peak and off-peak fares:

Tube, DLR, London Overground, TFL Rail and some National Rail services in London

• Peak fares apply Monday to Friday (not on public holidays) from 06:30 to 09:30 and 16:00 to 19:00.

• Off-peak fares apply at all other times and if you travel from a station outside Zone 1 to a station in Zone 1 between 16:00 and 19:00, Mondays to Fridays.

Bus & tram

The Pay As You Go fare on bus and tram is the same at all times, regardless of when you travel.

Bus & Tram Pass

A Bus & Tram Pass on your Oyster card allows you to travel when and where you like, as much as you like, on bus and tram services across London.

You can get a 7 Day, Monthly or Annual Bus & Tram Pass on Oyster. If you're using Oyster to Pay As You Go on bus and trams, there's a **flat-rate daily cap** regardless of when you travel.

Bus & Tram Passes don't have travel zones and are valid on all tram services and the entire London bus network, including some sections outside Greater London. Where you see the red roundel bus symbol displayed on a bus, you can use your Bus & Tram Pass.

If your Bus & Tram Pass is **valid** for longer than a month, your Oyster card will have to be registered. Registering your Oyster card also protects it against loss and **theft**. An Oyster card that has a Bus & Tram Pass on it can't be used by anyone other than the registered owner.

Words & Expressions

go credit 花销，赊账
tram /træm/ *n.* 有轨电车
DLR (Docklands Light Railway) 轻轨
overground 地上铁
TFL Rail 伦敦地铁
top up 充值
refund /rɪːˈfʌnd/ *v.* 退还；偿还
　　　　　　　　n. 退款

deduct /dɪˈdʌkt/ *v.* 扣除；演绎
maximum pay 最大支付额
flat-rate 统一收费
daily cap 每日上限
valid /ˈvælɪd/ *adj.* 有确实根据的，正当的，有效的
theft /θeft/ *n.* 偷窃，盗窃

M2-4

After reading, write T for True and F for False.

(　) 1. Oyster cards are used in London.
(　) 2. Oyster cards can only be used on the tube.
(　) 3. Passengers will pay the same with Oyster card and cash.
(　) 4. There are peak and off-peak fares with the Oyster card on any transportation tools.
(　) 5. Oyster cards can be protected from loss and theft only after registered.

Unit 2
Selling Tickets

What You Will Learn in This Unit

1. How to serve the guest to buy a ticket from a ticket vending machine.
2. How to reply to the guest from the ticket office.

Part I　Getting Started

1. The following are some pictures of machines in the metro. Can you write their right English names below?

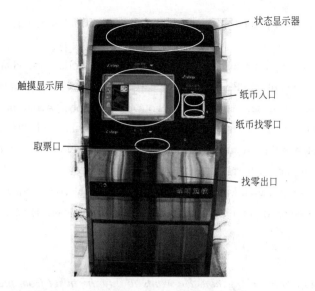

2. Can you explain the process of buying a ticket from a vending machine in English?

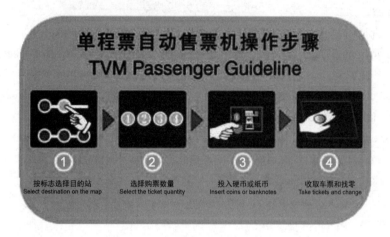

Part II Studying

A. Conversations

Conversation 1

Jack is a newcomer to Hangzhou. He wants to take the metro to the West Lake from Hangzhou Railway Station. Now he's in East Railway Station.

Jack: Excuse me.

Metro staff: Yes. What can I do for you?

M2-5

Jack: I'm new here. I want to buy a ticket to the West Lake from the machine?

Metro staff: OK, I will show you.

First, you should find your destination on the digital map on the screen and touch it like this. And then choose how many tickets you need on the right side. After that, the machine will show how much you should pay and the acceptable currency, coin or note. Next, you can put your notes here or coins in this slot. Wait several seconds, then the ticket and the change will fall to the tray here. Is that clear?

Jack: Thank you so much. By the way, if I want to recharge my traffic card, what should I do then?

Metro staff: First press the button "Recharging the card" on the screen. And then put your traffic card in card reader area. Here, you see. You will find your balance sheet. At the bottom, you can choose how much you want to recharge. There are 10 yuan, 20 yuan, 50 yuan and 100 yuan to choose. At last, put your bill in the slot, and the machine will recharge the card for you. After it's done, the screen will show the information of your recharging.

Jack: Well. It's a little complicated. I will try it now. Thank you for your kindness.

Metro staff: It's my pleasure. If you have other questions, ask me please. Bye!

Jack: Bye-bye!

Conversation 2

Jack is planning to go around Hangzhou. He wants to buy the ticket from the ticket office and ask more information about the city.

M2-6

Jack: Excuse me?

Metro staff: Yes, please. What can I do for you?

Jack: I'd like to go around Hangzhou today by metro. Could you tell me what kind of ticket I should buy?

Metro staff: You can choose tourist tickets, one-day pass or three-day pass. They are very convenient.

Jack: Could you tell me some more details?

Metro staff: For example, if you buy a one-day pass, you can go anywhere by the ticket no matter the lines, distance, and frequency. It's valid within 24 hours after you first use it.

Jack: Oh, marvelous. I will take one. How much is it?

Metro staff: Which one? One-day pass or three-day pass?

Jack: One-day pass.

Metro staff: It's 15 yuan for one.

Jack: Here you are.

(Jack gives a 50-yuan bill to the staff.)

Metro staff: Wait a minute. Here you are. This is the ticket and the change.

Jack: Thank you.

Metro staff: You are welcome. Have a nice day.

(Jack doesn't leave the station. He meets another staff and asks about some information about tourist attractions.)

Jack: Hello, may I ask you some questions?

Metro staff: Of course. What can I do for you?

Jack: I'd like to have some local food, such as snacks. Where should I go?

Metro staff: Now we are in Qianjiang Road. You can take Line 4 to Jinjiang and transfer to Line 1 and get off at Dingan Road.

Jack: Thank you so much.

Metro staff: Hold on a second. I can give you a metro map and show you.

Jack: Thanks a lot. You are so kind.

(After a while, the staff takes out a map and shows it to Jack.)

B. Words & Expressions

target /ˈtɑːgɪt/ n. 目标
complicated /ˈkɒmplɪkeɪtɪd/ adj. 复杂的
distance /ˈdɪstəns/ n. 距离；路程；
frequency /ˈfriːkwənsi/ n. 频率；发生次数
marvelous /ˈmɑːvələs/ adj. 非凡的；不可思议的
local /ˈləʊkl/ adj. 地方的；当地的
snack /snæk/ n. 小吃，快餐，点心

newcomer 新来的人
map of screen 屏幕上的地图
acceptable currency 可接受的币种
card reader area 读卡区
tourist ticket 旅游票
one-day pass 一日票

M2-7

C. Notes

1. 您好，您可以购买单程票。

Hello, you can buy a one-way ticket here.

2. 您好，您可以办理天府通卡。

Hello, you can get a Tianfu card here.

3. 您好，请问您到哪里？

Hello, which station are you heading to?

4. ××站一张，收您×元。

One ticket for ×× Station is × yuan.

5. 请拿好，找您零钱，谢谢。

Here is your ticket and your change. Thank you.

6. 这个问题请咨询站台值班人员（恐怕我不能回答这个问题）。

Please ask a station staff member about this question (I'm afraid I can't answer this question).

Part III Your Turn

A. Speaking Practice

1. Role Play

Take one of the roles according to the situation provided.

Student A: It's your first journey to China. You are in Beijing. Now you are in a metro station and eager to buy a ticket to Tian'anmen Square. You want to buy a ticket from a ticket vending machine.

Student B: You are a staff member in Beijing metro station. You are ready to help passengers.

Exchange roles

Student A: You are waiting to buy a ticket from the ticket office in Shanghai. You are wondering how to get to Shanghai Science & Technology Museum.

Student B: You are a staff member in Shanghai metro station. You are ready to help passengers.

2. Find appropriate expressions to show the meaning of the following pictures.

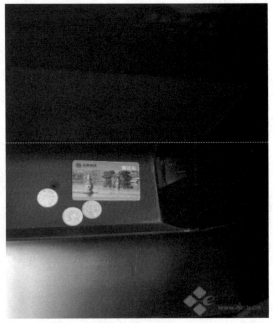
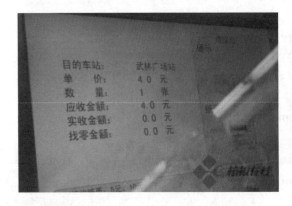

3. Group work

Do the following task in groups according to the requirement.

Do a survey of the metro in your city and make clear about all ticket fares and metro maps. Buy a ticket from a vending machine and find some questions or problems a foreign guest may face and report to the class.

B. Reading Practice

Read the passage and answer the questions that follow.

Which New York City Metro MetroCard to Buy

One question we often hear from our guests is which New York City metro MetroCard to buy, whether they should purchase an unlimited or a **pay-per-ride** MetroCard. The smallest pass is a weekly pass, and while it is relatively inexpensive, it leaves the possibility that you will be **donating** some money to the Metro Transit Authority (MTA). The answer really depends on a few factors.

First, let's breakdown the differences between the different MetroCards.

Unlimited Cards

- costs $31 for a 7-day pass and provides great savings
- for 13 trips = $2.38/ride
- for 20 trips = $1.55/ride
- for 25 trips = $1.24/ride
- can only be used by 1 person
- must wait 18 minutes before using again
- unlimited transfers

Pay-Per-Ride

- Costs $2.75/ride when you purchase multiple rides, otherwise it costs $3 per ride.
- 11% bonus for every $5.50 purchased. So, a $5.50 purchase gives you $6.10.
- Free metro-bus and bus-bus transfers within 2 hours. Metro to metro transfers are included within the system.
- Up to 4 people can use one MetroCard.
- **Seniors** are **eligible** for **discounts**.

For both types of cards, there is a $1 charge to obtain your MetroCard. If you are buying a pay-per-ride MetroCard, be sure to keep your card refilled when you top up, so to avoid the additional $1 charge. Often visitors are in the city for only 3 or 4 days. The main question you need to ask is whether you think you will use the card at least 12 times. If so, then the unlimited card will likely save you money. You are likely to use the metro at least 2 times per day, but you could use it at least 5 days if you were on our All-in-One Tour. If you like to take taxis, then having a pay-per-ride MetroCard may be your best choice.

For tips on how to actually use the MetroCard, we have provided a video **tutorial**.

Don't Do It Alone: Our New York Metro Art Tour, our All-in-One Tour as well as our Manhattan Night Tours use the metro and are part metro immersion courses and a great way to **familiarize** yourself with the New York metro System. For more information on MetroCards, visit the MTA website.

Words & Expressions

pay-per-ride 按次计卡
donate /dəʊˈneɪt/ v. 捐献，捐赠
senior /ˈsiːnɪə(r)/ n. 较年长者；上司；前辈；学长
eligible /ˈelɪdʒəbl/ adj. 符合条件的；合格的

discount /ˈdɪskaʊnt/ n. 折扣
v. 打折
tutorial /tjuːˈtɔːrɪəl/ n. 个别指导
familiarize /fəˈmɪliəraɪz/ v. 使熟悉，使熟知

M2-8

Questions

1. What is the price of a 7-day pass? Is it fit for a tourist traveling for 3 days? Why or why not?
2. How many persons can use one 7-day pass?
3. Why is pay-per-ride MetroCard convenient sometimes?
4. Can you write an advertisement to introduce your MetroCard fares?

Unit 3
The Excess Fare

What You Will Learn in This Unit

1. The excess fare for over-travel
2. The excess fare for overtime
3. The excess fare for children

Part I   Getting Started

Try to answer the questions using your knowledge.

1. Do you know how long a ticket allows a passenger to travel on the train, until they are required to pay the excess fare? How much should they pay?
2. Can passengers get out of station beyond their ticket limit? If it happens, what should you do?
3. Do you know the policy for lost tickets? List some of them in English.

Part II   Studying

A. Conversations

Conversation 1

Mr Smith suggested his family to visit Yuanmingyuan Imperial Garden. They will take the metro from Xidan to Yuanmingyuan Imperial Garden. When they arrive at the station, they realize that they left their commute cards in the luggage. Then, after Mr Smith goes through the turnstile, he gives his wife his commute card but the machine does not accept the card.

M2-9

SM: Excuse me, Sir. One commute card is applied to only one person for every single trip. Please go to the ticket center or a ticket machine to buy a ticket for this lady.

Mr Smith goes off to buy the ticket for his wife. They are now on the metro and discuss the weather of Beijing.

Smith: Oh, God! We missed our stop.

His wife: What? Can we just get off at another station and take another train back?

Smith: We can just get off at Xiyuan. It also has a nice view. The park is called the Summer Palace with great corridors and a lake. We can just go there first and then to Yuanmingyuan Imperial Garden. They are very close.

His wife: Good idea! Let's go there.

After they get off the metro, the turnstile won't let them get out.

SM: Excuse me. There's not enough credit on your tickets. Please go to the ticket center.

Mr Smith goes to the ticket center. A Metro staff checks their tickets and asks them to pay the excess fare for over-travel.

SM: Hello. You should pay two yuan for each, for you got off at a station beyond the ticket limit.

Smith: That's fine. Here you are.

After that, they get out of the station. What a messy day for them!

Conversation 2

Rose took her kid to the metro in Wangfujing after shopping. Her kid is only 10 years old, but she's 1.4 meters tall. Rose didn't buy a ticket for her daughter.

Rose: Follow me! When the door is open, let's run into it.

Kid: OK!

They're giggling.

Rose swiped the card on the turnstile machine. The door was open. They were ready to run. At the moment, the metro staff noticed.

SM: Excuse me, Madam. You can't do like this.

Rose: Why? She's my daughter. She's only 10 years old.

SM: Sorry. We have a policy that the child over 1.2 meters is required to buy a ticket.

Rose: OK, then I will get a ticket for her. No problem.

Rose and her daughter arrived at Yu Quanlu. They were exiting the turnstile but the daughter cannot insert her ticket into the slot because it was bent up. When they were on the metro, the girl was folding the card for fun.

Rose: Uh, what are you doing? Put your card into it like this.

Her daughter: My ticket is bent up like this.

She showed the bent card to her mother.

Rose: Oh, my! What should we do?

SM: You have to buy a new ticket to replace this one. May I ask where you're coming from?

Rose: Wangfujing.

SM: Okay. Please wait a second.

SM: Hello, it's the ticket. Next time, please take good care of your child.

Rose: Thank you very much. I won't allow her to do like that.

After exiting the station, Rose began to teach the kid the rules.

B. Words & Expressions

M2-11

suggest /sə'dʒest/ *v.* 提议，建议
realize /'rɪəlaɪz/ *v.* 领悟，认识到，了解
turnstile /'tɜːnstaɪl/ *n.* 十字转门；旋杆
corridor /'kɒrɪdɔː/ *n.* 走廊，回廊
credit /'kredɪt/ *n.* 信用、存款
beyond /bɪ'jɒnd/ *prep.* 超过
follow /'fɒləʊ/ *v.* 跟随，遵循，沿行；跟随；接着
giggle /'gɪgl/ *v.* 咯咯地笑
policy /'pɒlɪsi/ *n.* 政策，方针
require /rɪ'kwaɪə(r)/ *v.* 需要，要求，命令
exit /'eksɪt/ *v.* 退出；出去

insert /ɪn'sɜːt/ *v.* 插入；嵌入；放入
fold /fəʊld/ *v.* 折叠；交叠，交叉；对折
replace /rɪ'pleɪs/ *v.* 以……代替；取代
rule /ruːl/ *n.* 规则，惯例
miss the stop 坐过站
excess fare 超乘费
over-travel 超乘
ticket limit 票价限制
swipe the card 刷卡
bent up 弯曲

C. Notes

1. 可以在地铁车站的自动售票机和车站"票务中心"办理充值业务。
You may recharge your card at the ticket machine or the ticket center.

2. 非地铁方面原因，车票售出后概不退换。
There is no refund after purchase except under certain circumstances that are the result of some technical errors from the metro.

3. 车票只有当日有效，若丢失请补票。
The ticket is valid only on the day of purchase. If you lose the ticket, you should pay the excess one.

4. 不好意思，您的车票超乘了，请补足车费。
I'm sorry but your card is no longer valid because you got off at a different station. You will have to pay for the over-travel.

5. 您的票超时了，你需要补足3元超时费。
I'm sorry but your card is no longer valid because it is beyond the allowable time period. You will have to pay 3 yuan for the overtime fee.

6. 对不起，您的小孩超高1.2米，需要补一张单程票。
I'm sorry but your child is taller than 1.2 meters. He/She will need to buy a ticket.

Part III Your Turn

A. Writing Practice

1. Match the following English sentences with their corresponding Chinese ones.

1) The ticket machine only accepts 5-yuan notes, 10-yuan notes and 1-yuan coins.

2) You may recharge your card at the vending machine.

3) Hello, please choose your destination station.

4) Please select the number of tickets.

5) Please collect your ticket and change at the tray on the bottom.

6) This way, please.

7) I'm sorry. This ticket machine is short of change. Please use another one.

8) Please come here to refund your ticket.

A. 您好，请选择您的目的站。

B. 请从取票口取走您的车票。

C. 自动售票机可接受5元、10元纸币，1元硬币。

D. 不好意思，本机零钱不足，请到其他机器购票。

E. 请到这边办理退票业务。

F. 请选择你购买的张数。

G. 请您往这边进站。

H. 自动售票机可以充值你的卡。

2. Can you explain the following policies in English?

（1）超时乘车规定

乘客每次乘车从入闸到出闸时限为120分钟。超过120分钟，须按最高单程票价补交超时车费。

（2）超程乘车规定

乘客所使用的车票，不足以支付所到达车站的实际车费时，须补交超程车费。

（3）超时、超程乘车规定

乘客乘坐一个车程既超时又超程，须按最高单程票价补交超时车费。

持免费票或地铁方面的原因，在超时、超程条件下无须补交车费。

（4）遗失车票规定

a. 乘客在付费区内遗失储值车票，须到车站票务处按最高单程票价补票。

b. 乘客在付费区内遗失免费票，须交车票制作工本费3元，然后免费给予出站。

c. 乘客在付费区内遗失单程票，须交车票制作工本费3元，然后按最高单程票价补票后给予出站。

B. Speaking Practice

Student A acts as a passenger from Boston who lost the ticket on the metro. Student B acts as a metro staff to explain the policy and guide the passenger to deal with the problem.

C. Reading Practice

Read the following passage and answer the questions below.

Card Replacement Basics

If your **registered** SmarTrip card was lost, stolen, or damaged, then the **remaining balance** may be transferred from the old card to a new card for the cost of a new card. If it **malfunctioned** and showed no sign of damage, then Metro will also **reimburse** you for the cost of a **replacement card**. See the Registered SmarTrip Card Replacement section for more details.

If your unregistered SmarTrip card or your farecard/pass has become damaged or is malfunctioning, then obtain a **signed fare adjustment envelope** from a Metrorail station manager and follow the instructions.

If you need a replacement right away, then you may purchase your card from a SmarTrip **dispenser** in any Metrorail station or at any Metro sales location. Contact Metro Customer Assistance at 202-637-7000 if you need additional assistance.

Metro is not responsible for farecards, passes, **tokens** or unregistered SmarTrip cards that are lost or stolen.

If you are unable to present the evidence of fare payment at a Metrorail exit, then you must see the Station Manager. The maximum fare may be charged based on the time of exit.

Words & Expressions

register /ˈredʒɪstə(r)/ n. 清单，记录
　　　　　　　　　　 v. 登记，注册
remaining balance 余额
malfunction /ˌmælˈfʌŋkʃn/ n.& v. 发生故障，不起作用
reimburse /ˌriːɪmˈbɜːs/ v. 偿还；赔偿
replacement card 替换卡

signed fare adjustment envelope 已签署的票价调整信封
dispenser /dɪˈspensə(r)/ n. 自动售货机
token /ˈtəʊkən/ n. 代币，辅币；代价券；礼券

M2-12

Questions

1. Can you find some familiar words we have learned before? List them.
2. What should a passenger do if he/she damages an unregistered card?
3. What should a passenger do if he/she can't present the card or fare payment?

Unit 4
Ticket Policy

What You Will Learn In This Unit

1. Free tickets for the disabled, soliders and the old
2. How to solve invalid tickets
3. How to deal with the problem of receipts

Part I　Getting Started

Try to answer the questions using your knowledge.

1. Can you distinguish the following persons and list who can get concessionary fares?

2. Group discussion.

What's the policy for concessionary fares in your city?

Part II Studying

A. Conversations

Conversation 1

Michelle came to Chengdu, and she noticed there's a notice on the metro entrance. She was curious about it and asked a metro worker to explain to her.

Michelle: Excuse me? Can you explain something on the notice?

Metro Worker: Of course.

M2-13

It's about the policy for concessionary fares. In Chengdu, the servicemen, disabled veterans and the blind can get free tickets. Children under 1.2 meters high can also enjoy the policy. However, one adult can only take one child for free, and other children along should buy tickets.

Michelle: It's reasonable. However, I am wondering if you give any privileges to senior citizens. I'm 70 years old now.

Staff: We offer free rides to senior citizens over 70. However, the time is restricted to non-rush hours and it should be registered on his/her Tianfu Card. If you want to register for it, you can go to the public service center in any districts and ask more information about it.

Michelle: Thank you so much. Bye.

Staff: See you.

Conversation 2

Lisa took the Nanjing metro one day, but she lost her ticket on the train. After she got to the destination, she hurried to ask the staff member for help.

Lisa: Excuse me, can you help me?

SM: Yes, Madam. What's wrong?

M2-14

Lisa: I lost my ticket on the train. I can't find it now. Can you help me?

SM: Is your ticket a registered card or a recycled card from the vending machine?

Lisa: I just bought it in Zhonghuamen Station.

SM: That's too bad. You'd better go to the ticket office to repay the ticket.

Lisa: How much should I pay indeed?

SM: If anyone loses the ticket, he or she must pay from the beginning station to here. That's to say,

you have to pay 4 yuan from Mai'aoqiao Station.
Lisa: But I didn't go so far.
SM: I'm so sorry. It's our policy and thank you for your cooperation.
Lisa: I should be careful next time.
SM: Yes, sorry again.

B. Words & Expressions

notice / ˈnəʊtɪs/ *n.* 注意，通知，布告
entrance /ˈentrəns/ *n.* 入口，门口
curious /ˈkjʊərɪəs/ *adj.* 好奇的；古怪的；求知的
concessionary /kənˈseʃənəri/ *adj.* 减价的；优惠的
blind /blaɪnd/ *adj* 瞎的
privilege / ˈprɪvəlɪdʒ/ *n.* 特权，特别恩典
offer /ˈɒfə(r)/ *v.* 提供，贡献，出价
restrict /rɪˈstrɪkt/ *v.* 限制，限定，约束
district /ˈdɪstrɪkt/ *n.* 区域，地方
repay / rɪˈpeɪ/ *v.* 偿还；付还；再次付钱
indeed /ɪnˈdiːd/ *adv.* 真正地；当然；确实
cooperation /kəʊˌɒpəˈreɪʃn/ *n.* 合作，协力

concessionary fare 优惠票
serviceman 现役军人
disabled veteran 残疾军人
take sb for free 带某人免费（进入）
a free ride 免费乘坐
public service center 公共服务中心
lose the ticket 丢了票
a registered card 已经注册的卡
a recycled card 循环卡
the beginning station 起始站

M2-15

C. Notes

1. 我们会给你提供一张免费票，你就用这张票出闸吧。
We will issue you a new ticket to get out. There will be no charge for this one.
2. 义务兵、伤残军人、残疾人民警察、盲人、其他重度残疾人免费乘坐。
Servicemen, disabled veterans and disabled policemen, the blind, and other passengers with severe disabilities enjoy free rides.
3. 每位成年人可免费携带一名身高1.2米以下儿童乘车。
Any adult can brings a child under 1.2 meters for free.
4. 纪念票、其他特殊票种。
Commemorative tickets, other special tickets.
5. 我们这里暂时不提供发票。
We can't offer receipts temporarily.
6. 您可以到售票窗口去取发票。
You can get a receipt from the ticket center.

Part III   Your Turn

A. Speaking Practice

1. Role Play

Student A acts as a metro worker, and student B acts as a foreign guest who has some ticket troubles.

Sample A
The foreign guest can't get out from the turnstile because the credit on his card is not enough for the distance.

Sample B
The foreign guest lost his wallet including his ticket on the train. He can't get out of the station.

2. Can you translate the following policy of excess fares into English?

补票规则：

a. 乘客所使用的车票，不足以支付所到达车站的实际车费时，须在车站人工售票亭办理补票手续方可出站。

b. 乘客从进闸到出闸时间超过2小时，须在车站人工售票亭按出闸站线网单程最高票价补交超时车费后方可出站。

c. 乘客在出闸时无票或车票损坏，须在车站人工售票亭按出闸站线网单程最高票价补交车费。

d. 乘客持天府通卡出站时卡内余额不足，须在车站人工售票亭办理充值业务后，持原卡扣费出站；或在购买出站票后免费更新原卡，持出站票出站。

B. Reading Practice

Read the following passage and answer the questions below.

Singapore Child Concession Card

What is it?

A **Child Concession Card** is similar to an Adult Stored Value card but made for children to travel for free/at concessionary prices!

With the enhanced concession scheme kicking in on 6 April 2014, children under 7 years old can travel for **FREE** on basic bus services, express bus services and trains.

Please take note that concessionary fares are not applicable on **Premium bus services**, and NightRider services.

Existing cardholders may continue to use their current card to enjoy privileges from 6 April 2014.

How do I know if my child is eligible for the card?

If your child is above 0.9m in height, below 7 years old and not in primary school, you may apply for a Child Concession Card. The card will be valid for use till 30 April of the year the child turns 7 years old.

All children up to 0.9m in height and **accompanied** by a fare-paying **commuter** will travel for free from 6 April 2014.

Oh that's nice! But how do I apply for one?

If your child is a Singapore Citizen or a Singapore **Permanent Resident**, simply click here to download the form. Then **submit** the completed forms to any TransitLink Ticket Office with the child's details such as full name, Birth Certificate Number and date of birth. The parent or **proxy** making the purchase is required to produce his/her NRIC.

If your child is a non-Singapore Citizen or non-Singapore Permanent Resident, remember to bring along your child's Passport (**photocopy** or **original** is accepted) when purchasing the Child Concession Card.

The card will **be encoded with** the child's name, Birth Certificate/Passport number, date of birth and **expiry date** of the card. Each eligible child **is entitled to** purchase one Child Concession Card.

Words & Expressions

Child Concession Card 儿童优惠卡
premium bus service 高端汽车服务
accompany /əˈkʌmpəni/ v. 陪伴，伴随；伴奏
commuter /kəˈmjuːtə(r)/ n. 通勤者，经常乘公共车辆往返者；[交] 月季票乘客
permanent resident 永久居民
submit /səbˈmɪt/ v. 使服从；主张；呈递；提交
proxy /ˈprɒksi/ n. 代理人；委托书；代用品

photocopy /ˈfəʊtəʊkɒpi/ n. 复印件 v. 影印
original /əˈrɪdʒənl/ n. 原件，原版
be encoded with 被赋予；天生具有
expiry date 到期日
be entitled to 有权；有……的资格

M2-16

Questions

1. What is the Chinese name of Concession Card?
2. Who can get a concession card in Singapore?
3. What information is needed to register a card like this?
4. What services are excluded from the concession card?

Chapter Three
Information Signs of Metro Stations

Learning Outcomes

On completion of the module, you will be able to:
1. Understand different signs of metro stations
2. Express different names of stations and distance
3. Introduce facilities for the handicapped

Overview of the Module

  The sign in the station is one of the most important metro cultures, which presents the complex information with simple pictures. It's a kind of visual expression widely applied in different areas. The passengers can follow the sign to do the operation or enter/exit the gate successfully.

  As a staff member in the metro, one must accurately remember the names of different stations and their different distance. The staff should also know and explain to the passengers how to transfer to other transportation tools in order to reach the landmarks.

  A qualified staff member should be a good helper for anyone in need, especially for the disabled. They should explain the location of facilities to the handicapped and help them to go through them.

Unit 1
Signs in Metro Station

What You Will Learn in This Unit

1. Common signs in metro stations
2. Information of different stations

Part I Getting Started

1. The following are the different signs. Write down the English translations below.

2. How many metro lines are there in your city? Do you know the names of all metro stations? Exchange your knowledge about them with your partner and then draw a map of metro lines together. Don't forget to mark all the stations in English.

Part II Studying

A. Conversations

Conversation 1

Jenny and her little brother Tom are playing hide-and-seek nearby the platform in a metro station.

SM: Hello, kids. Can you stop for a while?

Jenny: What? Why?

SM: Did you notice there's a sign on the wall?

(The staff member points at the sign and explains.)

SM: It's very dangerous to play in the station. You know the train runs at a high speed. If your brother fell down onto the railway, we could do nothing. It's horrible.

(At that time, Jenny's mother, Mary, walks towards the children.)

Mary: What's up?

SM: Madam, please take care of your children. It's prohibited to play in the station, because there are large crowds of people and fast trains.

Mary: Sorry, I will ask them to keep quiet. Sorry to trouble you.

SM: Thank you for your cooperation.

M3-1

Conversation 2

Jack and his friends have just came back from Lhasa. Mr Brown will go to the airport to pick up them. He is now at Peking University Station. He doesn't know how to get to the airport by metro.

Metro worker: Hello, can I help you?
Mr Brown: Yes. I will go to the airport. Can you please tell me how to get there?
Metro worker: You can take Line 4 to Xizhimen, and then transfer to Line 2 to Dongzhimen. When you arrive there, you don't need to get out of the station. You can directly take the airport express there.
Mr Brown: Oh, it's so complicated.
Metro worker: If you're not sure how to get there, you can ask another metro worker for help once you get off at Dongzhimen Station.
Mr Brown: How long will it take me there?
Metro worker: Around 50 minutes.
Mr Brown: Thank you. You are really helpful.
Metro worker: It's my pleasure. Have a nice ride, Sir.
Mr Brown: Thanks.

B. Words & Expressions

sign /saɪn/ n. 标志；招牌；标牌
dangerous /ˈdeɪndʒərəs/ adj. 危险的
horrible /ˈhɒrəbl/ adj. 可怕的，极可憎的
prohibit /prəˈhɪbɪt/ v. 禁止，阻止
crowd /kraʊd/ n. 人群
　　　　　　v. 挤，拥挤

directly /dɪˈrektlɪ/ adv. 直接地；坦率地
run at a high speed 高速行驶
hide-and-seek 捉迷藏
what's up? 什么事？
airport express 机场快线

C. Notes

1. 我迷路了。
I'm lost.
2. ……站在哪儿？
Where is _____ Station?
3. 我该怎样去……站？
How can I get to _____ Station?
4. 请问到……应该在哪个地铁站下车？
Could you tell me which station should I get off if I go to _____?
5. ……出口在哪里？哪个出口能到……？
Where is the Exit _____? /
Which is the exit to _____?
6. 去……是这个方向吗？
Is this the right way to _____?

7. 卫生间在哪里？
Where is the toilet/restroom/washroom?
8. 乘坐……号线到……站
Take Line _____ to _____ Station.
9. 转……号线
Transfer to Line _____.
10. 在……站下车
You can get off at _____ Station.
11. 在……大街/路/大道
It's on _____ Street/Road/Avenue.
12. 在……和……的拐角处
It's at the corner of _____ and _____.

13. 在银行/医院/购物中心/学校的旁边
It's next to the bank/hospital/mall/school.
14. 在……的对面
It's across from the _____.
15. 在书店的对面
It's opposite the bookstore.
16. 沿着……路到……街

Go down _____ Road to _____ Street.
17. 在……大道左转
Turn left on _____ Street.
18. 就在你的右边/左边
It's on your right/left.
19. 正好在你前面
It will be in front of you.

Part III　Your Turn

A. Speaking Practice

1. One foreign guest wants to smoke in the station. What should you tell him? Have a role play with your partner to show it out.

2. The following is a metro map of Shanghai. Please describe how a passenger can travel from Shanghai Railway Station to Pudong Airport.

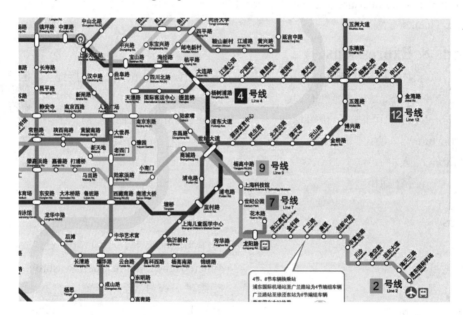

B. Reading Practice

Read the following signs and do the following exercises.

Questions

1. Can you translate all the signs into Chinese and explain them to the passengers?

2. Can you find the proper words to describe the pictures above?

Unit 2
Station Names and the Distance

What You Will Learn in This Unit

1. Names of stations and translation skills
2. Platform announcements

Part I Getting Started

望京东	A. Wangjingdong	B. Wangjing East
北苑	A. Beiyuan	B. North Garden
生物医药基地	A. Shengwu Yiyao Jidi	B. Biomedical Base

| 小红门 | A. Small Red Door | B. Xiao Hongmen |
| 人民大学 | A. Renming University | B. People's University |

1. Make a judgment of the following translation of station names.

Tips：中国街道名称的英译方法，目前大体上有三大类：一是"汉语拼音法"，二是"音意结合法"，三是"全盘意译法"。"汉语拼音法"即用汉语拼音来处理中国街道名称的英译，例如："亮马河南路"英译为"Liangmahe Nanlu"，"东直门外大街"英译为"Dongzhimenwai Dajie"，"北十九道街"英译为"Beishijiudao Jie"，等；有的还将每一个汉字单独译为一个词，如："光华路"译为"Guang Hua Lu"。"音意结合法"是指将专名部分作音译处理，通名部分作意译处理，这是比较流行的译法。如："城中路"译为"Chengzhong Road"，"民主街"译成"Minzhu Street"；另外在"路""街"之前，还设有"大、干、正""东、西、南、北""上、中、下""前、后、内、外""支、横、新、旧""一、二、三"等。有的则称"路"为"道"，这时将"大道""大街"译为"Main Road""Main Street"，有时统译为"Avenue"，或译为法语的"Boulevard"，或直接译为"Road"和"Street"。如"沙面大街"译为"Shamian Street"。对"东、西、南、北、中"的处理，可以把这些方位词分别放在前、中、后的位置上，如：同一条"天宁南路"就有"South Tianning Road""Tianning South Road"和"Tianning Road South"三种译法。也有将"东、西、南、北、中"并入专名部分的译法，如：将"解放中路"译为"Jiefangzhong Road"。对"前、后、内、外""上、下""支、新"的处理比较多样。如"水西门外江东门新街"译为"New Street, Jiangdong Gate, Outside Shuixi Gate"，有的将"外"译为"Outer"。对于"里、巷、弄"，三者均可译成"lane""alley"或"alleyway"。如"向阳一巷"译为"Xiangyang Alley No.1"。也有拼音化的，如"大众巷"译成"Dazhong Xiang"。"全盘意译法"就是彻底的意译法。如"五一路"译为"May 1st Road"，"天坛路"译为"Temple of Heaven Road"，"珠江路"译为"Pearl River Road"，甚至将"经四纬六路"译为"Longitude 4 Latitude 6 Road"，等等。

2. Translate the following announcement into Chinese.

Dear passengers, the train is bound for Xiaogang. The next station is Changgang. You can transfer to Line 2. Passengers who need to get off, please get ready! Please mind the gap between the train and the platform.

Part II　Studying

A. Conversations

Conversation 1

Jack couldn't understand some station names in Guangzhou. He discussed with one of his Chinese students, Li Hao.

Jack: Li Hao. It's so confusing for me to remember the names of Guangzhou metro stations.

Li Hao: Can you list some names?

Jack: Chebeinan and Chebei. I wonder whether there might be some connection between the names.

Li Hao: Yes, Chebeinan is on the south of Chebei.

Jack: So it should be South Chebei.

M3-4

Li Hao: Jack, can you tell me how to translate the name of places?

Jack: Generally, the direction on the name should be translated as its original meaning, such as north, south, east or west. Secondly, some common names, such as Road, Avenue or Bridge, should also be translated into what kind of Road. Take Beijing Hua Yuanqiao as an example. It should be translated as Hua Yuan Bridge. Another name in Beijing is "HUIXINXIJIENANKOU". What's that? How funny!

Li Hao: Maybe you are talking about "惠新西街南口". Actually, I think it should be "South End of West Huixi Street". However, it's too long.

Jack: The name of stations should accord with the pronunciation of English. How can we read the long name?

Li Hao: Yes. Nice to talk with you.

Jack: See you.

Conversation 2

Mary and her kid Jack were on the metro.

Jack: Mother, what's the announcer saying?

Mary: She says the next station is Convention & Exhibition Center, we can transfer to Longhua Line.

Jack: I see. And then what's the meaning of the next one as we were on the platform just now.

Mary: I'm not sure.

Jack: Listen. She is saying it again.

Mary: Oh, she says disembarking precedes embarking.

Jack: What does it mean?

Mary: It means we should be polite to others. When the door is open, we should let others get off the train in advance. Then we can get on the train. It's a formal word.

Jack: Mother, I also find their English names very interesting, such as Gouwugongyuan. What's that?

Mary: It's a park maybe. The writing form is Pinyin. Probably they think when a foreigner is asking the way, it's more convenient for the local people to understand and give a hand.

Jack: But it's weird. It's really hard to remember the long name.

Mary: It's part of Chinese culture.

B. Words & Expressions

confusing /kənˈfjuːzɪŋ/ *adj.* 令人困惑的
connection /kəˈnekʃn/ *n.* 联系，关联；联结
translate /trænsˈleɪt/ *v.* 翻译，转化
direction /dɪˈrekʃn/ *n.* 方向；趋势
common /ˈkɒmən/ *adj.* 通常的，通俗的
avenue /ˈævənjuː/ *n.* 大街，林荫路；途径
accord /əˈkɔːd/ *v.* 调解，使一致
pronunciation /prəˌnʌnsiˈeɪʃn/ *n.* 发音，读音
announcer /əˈnaʊnsə(r)/ *n.* 报幕员，广播员

disembark /ˌdɪsɪmˈbɑːk/ *v.* 下车
precede /prɪˈsiːd/ *v.* 在……之前，较……优先
embark /ɪmˈbɑːk/ *v.* 上车，上船；使从事
formal /ˈfɔːml/ *adj.* 正式的
Chinese culture 中国文化
north, south, east or west 北、南、东或西

C. Notes

1. **Convention & Exhibition Center**：深圳会展中心，该中心是集展览、会议、商务、餐饮、娱乐等多种功能为一体的超大型公共建筑，由深圳市政府投资兴建，德国GMP公司设计，总投资32亿人民币。会展中心总建筑面积28万平方米，东西长540米，南北宽282米，总高60米，地上六层，地下三层。深圳会展中心是深圳市最大的单体建筑，是钢结构与玻璃穹顶及幕墙的结合体。

2. 本次列车开往……方向。

This train is bound for/goes to/runs to _____.

3. 本次列车终点站为……

This train stops at ____.

4. 左侧的车门将会打开。

Doors open on the left.

5. 请小心列车和站台之间的空隙。

Please mind the gap between the train and the platform.

6. 开往罗湖方向的列车即将进站，请勿靠近屏蔽门，请排队候车。

The train for Luohu is approaching, please keep clear of the door. Please line up.

7. 车门即将关闭，谨防夹伤。

The door is closing soon, please mind your hand.

Part III Your Turn

A. Speaking Practice

The following part is some announcements on the metro. Read and practice them with your local metro station names.

1. Welcome to take Beijing metro on your next trip. Have a nice day!

2. Welcome to metro Line 2. The next station is Zhongshan North Road. Please get ready for your arrival and get off in order.

3. Please stand firm and hold the handrail.

4. The train to Jingan Temple is arriving. Jingan Temple is a transfer station. Passengers for Line 2 please get off the train.

5. The door on the left side will be used, please take care and make sure you have all your belongings with you.

6. The train is arriving. Please mind the gap between the train and the platform.

7. This train will stop service at Anheqiao North Station.

B. Reading Practice

Read the following announcement and sense the difference among nations.

Voices in the Deep Departure sounds and next-station announcements in metro systems around the world.

It would be an **exaggeration** to say that one could learn languages by listening to metro announcements, but a visitor can at least get a good impression of the local language and its pronunciations from the **periodically** repeated announcements on trains.

Buffalo

The door-closing signal is a two to three second long series of harsh, fast, very high-pitched beeps (sounds like "scree-scree-scree-scree-scree..."), followed by a simple live announcement of the next station by the train driver. Every few stations, a live warning is announced: "No smoking, drinking, eating, playing of radio or tape players allowed in all metro vehicles and stations". The **sequence** and announcement wording are unchanged from the time the system opened in 1984.

Chicago

A very friendly, pre-recorded male voice talks almost **permanently** to the passengers: "[ding-dong] doors closing". "... Adams and Wabash is next. Doors open on the right at Adams and Wabash. Transfer to Green, Purple, and Brown Line trains at Adams and Wabash". "... This is Adams and Wabash. Transfer to Green, Purple, and Brown Line trains at Adams and Wabash. This is an Orange line train to Midway." And sometimes, one of the following is being added: "Standing passengers: please do not lean against the doors.", "**Priority seating** is intended for the elderly and passengers with disabilities. Your cooperation is requested.", "**Soliciting** on CTA trains is prohibited. **Violators** will be arrested.", "Smoking, littering, and playing radios or loud devices is prohibited.", "Your attention please. We are being delayed because crews are working on the track ahead. We expect to be moving shortly.", "Your attention please. We are being delayed, waiting for signals ahead. We expect to be moving shortly.", "Thank you for riding the CTA Orange Line." .

Dublin

DART: Doors: soft whistling/chirping noise before and during door closing. Lights also flash. On board (male voice): "This train is for: [final destination]". Chime, "Your attention please. The next station is [name]" — "This is [station name]". Other announcements (all prefixed with a chime followed by "Your attention please!"): "For your comfort and safety, please do not smoke or place your feet on the seats". "For your safety, CCTV is fitted on this train". LUAS: Doors: There's a soft tone and lights flash above every door before they close. A female voice "Doors are about to close" is sometimes used ahead of that announcement, particularly when departing from the end of the line. Stations: "The next stop is [station name]". On arrival at the stop "[station name]" in English and Gaelic. It will also add other information like "Change here for... " or "Last stop". Other announcements: "Thank you for traveling with LUAS". "Please keep your feet off the seats".

Kolkata

All announcements are in three languages—Bangla (local language), Hindi (national language) and English. The announcement is of the form "The next station is XYZ, the platform on the right/left." There are only beeps for closing doors, no announcements.

Chapter Three   Information Signs of Metro Stations   ▶▶ *045*

London	A faint chirping sound before the doors close. Announcements differ: Jubilee Line ("Please mind the doors"), Northern Line ("Stand back from the doors"), Bakerloo Line ("This train is about to depart, please mind the doors"; this is rarely said though), the rest just seem to make a beeping noise or on the Central Line just a loud kind of **screech**... When the train comes to a halt, there's sometimes the famous **recurring** "Mind the gap!" by an automated male voice, sometimes a single "Mind the gap between the train and the platform" by a female voice.
Mumbai	Metro: "Do-do-do-do-do-do-do-do..." until the doors close, similar to Hong Kong. Suburban Railway: no announcements. Monorail: Before the doors close, automated male voice: "Stand clear, doors closing!" Female voice: "Next station: [station name]. Please make way for **alighting** passengers!" Before the doors open at a station, female voice: "Doors opening. Please stand clear of the door!"
Philadelphia	On the Broad Street Line, the trains have two **chimes** at the same tone "[dong-dong]" and a two-tone chime before any announcements. The Market-Frankford Line has automated announcements that go something like this: "This is a 69th Street train making all stops. This is a Frankford train making A stops. A stops only! [same for B] Doors opening! Doors closing!"
Shanghai	Doors-closing signal is a "beep-beep-beep...", continued until the doors are closed and accompanied by flashing lights above the doors. Pre-recorded announcements on the ride: "Next station is [name]." Before the train stops, you hear in Mandarin Chinese "Arrived at station [name]", followed in English: "We are now at [name]."
Singapore	Announcements differ. Lines operated by SMRT: "Doors are closing", followed by about 15 ultra-short beeps (amr). "Next station, [name]", station announcements "[Name], [name]". At underground stations: "Please mind the platform gap". Lines operated by SBS Transit: "Doors closing", followed by short beeps. "Next station [English name], [Chinese name]."
Sydney	Sydney's **millennium** train goes like this: "Beep Beep Beep!"—"Please stand clear. Doors closing. Next stop, Town Hall. Get off at Town Hall for Queen Victoria Building and Darling Harbour". On other lines, most train sets have recorded announcements "Stand clear, doors closing" or the newer one "Doors closing, please stand clear," and in some train sets followed by different kinds of beeps. Some trains beep also when doors open. On the Illawarra Line, when it approaches a station, a female voice announces: "Next stop, [name]". For transfer stations it adds: "Passengers should change at [name] for services to [name]".

Washington D. C

An automated "Doors closing, [ding-dong]". A new type of announcement says: "Doors opening, step back to allow customers to exit. When boarding, please move to the center of the car.—[Ding-dong ding-dong] step back, doors closing!".

Words & Expressions

exaggeration /ɪɡˌzædʒəˈreɪʃn/ n. 夸张；夸大之词
periodically /ˌpɪəriˈɒdɪkli/ adv. 定期地；周期性地
sequence /ˈsiːkwəns/ n. [数][计] 序列；顺序；续发事件 v. 安排顺序
permanently /ˈpɜːmənəntli/ adv. 永久地，长期不变地
priority seating 优先座
solicit /səˈlɪsɪt/ v. 征求；招揽；请求；乞求
violator /ˈvaɪəleɪtə(r)/ n. 违背者；违反者

screech /skriːtʃ/ v. 尖叫；尖着声音地说；发出尖锐刺耳的声音
recurring /rɪˈkɜːrɪŋ/ adj. 循环的；再发的
alight /əˈlaɪt/ v. 从（公共汽车、火车等）下来
chime /tʃaɪm/ v. 鸣响；和谐；打钟报时；敲出和谐的声音
millennium /mɪˈleniəm/ n. 千年期（尤指公元纪年）；千周年纪念日；新千年开始的时刻

M3-7

Question

Discuss with your classmates about the announcement in different countries. What should Chinese stations do to improve the announcement?

Unit 3
Introduction of Facilities for the Handicapped

What You Will Learn in This Unit

1. Facilities for the handicapped
2. How to help the handicapped

Part I　Getting Started

1. Do you know the Chinese name and English name of the following facilities? Write their names on the lines.

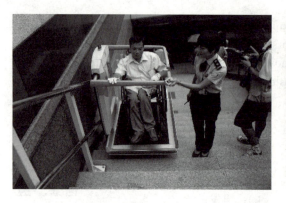

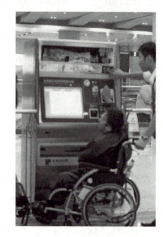

2. What are the different features of the disabled such as the blind, deaf, handicapped? What can we do for them?

Part II Studying

A. Conversation

Jack is a disabled person. He can't move his legs, so the wheelchair is his only way of transportation. Today he is trying to take the Beijing metro to see his friend in Peking University.

Jack: Excuse me?

Staff Member A: Yes? What can I do for you?

Jack: How can I go downstairs? The stairs are too dangerous for me.

Staff Member A: I will show you the way. Take the elevator over there, you will directly reach the ticket lobby.

Jack: Thank you so much!

Staff Member A: It's my pleasure.

M3-8

When they went to the ticket lobby, the staff explained the preferential policy to Jack, which is the free ticket for the disabled. Jack was very pleased at the policy and sensed the care to the disabled. The staff member opened the side gate for Jack and Jack went to the platform. Another one was on duty on the platform.

Staff Member B: Excuse me, Sir? What can I do for you?

Jack: Can I get on the train with my wheelchair?

Staff Member B: No problem. I will help you then.

Jack: Thank you!

Jack was waiting in the special area for the disabled on the platform. The train is coming.

Staff Member B: Excuse me! This passenger should get on board in advance. Thank you for your cooperation.

Staff Member B: You can wait in the zone only for the physically challenged. Hold on to the handrail.

Jack: Thank for your kindness.

Staff Member B: You are welcome.

When Jack got off the train, his friend was waiting for him outside. Jack immediately told his friend about the experience on the train.

B. Words & Expressions

wheelchair /'wi:ltʃeə(r)/ n. 轮椅
transportation /ˌtrænspɔː'teɪʃn/ n. 运输，交通
downstairs /ˌdaʊn'steəz/ adv. 在楼下；往楼下
stairs /steəz/ n. 楼梯
elevator /'elɪveɪtə(r)/ n. 电梯；升降机
lobby /'lɒbɪ/ n. 大厅；休息室
preferential /ˌprefə'renʃl/ adj. 优先的；优惠的；优待的
sense /sens/ v. 感到，认识，理解
zone /zəʊn/ n. 地带，地域，地区

physically /'fɪzɪklɪ/ adv. 身体上
challenge /'tʃælɪndʒ/ v. 向……挑战
kindness /'kaɪndnɪs/ n. 仁慈；好意；和蔼；友好的行为
immediately /ɪ'miːdɪətli/ adv. 立刻，立即
side gate 边门
on duty 值班
get on board 上车
in advance 提前；优先

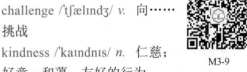
M3-9

C. Notes

1. free ride for the disabled：残疾人士凭中国残疾人联合会统一发放的"残疾人证"，可以免费乘坐公共电车、公共汽车。盲人朋友在免费乘坐公共电、汽车的基础上，还可以免费乘坐城市轨道交通。在盲人本人免费乘坐地铁的同时，还允许一名陪同人员一起免费乘坐地铁。具体实施细则各城市不同。

2. non-obstacle facilities：呼叫设备（help line）、可视对讲（visual-speaking system）、爬楼车（climbing car）、升降平台（lifting platform）、坡道（ramp）、直升电梯（elevator）、盲道（sidewalk for the blind）、无障碍厕所（wheelchair accessible toilet）、无障碍通道（barrier free access）、优先座位（priority seating）

3. 残疾人的英语称谓：残疾人的英语表达应该是 handicapped, disabled person, physically challenged。但是为了让对方感到亲切，称呼应该和正常人一样，称为 Sir, 或是 Madam。

Part III Your Turn

A. Speaking Practice

In this part, Student A will act as a disabled person and Student B will be a metro staff. Practice the greeting words and help the disabled successfully get on and off the train and use the facilities.

B. Reading Practice

Metro Accessibility Measures

- All Metrorail stations and rail cars are accessible.
- Accessible priority parking spaces near the rail station entrance are reserved for vehicles **displaying DMV handicapped** permits or **license plates**.
- Outside of rail stations, there are directional signs to the station's accessible entrance. There are also signs that identify the accessible elevator entrance.
- The information **pylon** outside of each Metro station includes information in Braille and raised alphabet.
- Most escalators in rail stations have bright **contrasting** paint at the edge of each step to assist people with low vision.
- Each rail station has an accessible fare vending machine with **lower panels**. Easy-to-use instructions are included in Braille and raised alphabet; there is also a button to press for **audio instructions**.
- Each Metro rail station entrance has an extra-wide, accessible faregate for customers who use wheelchairs, **scooters**, and other mobility devices. The farecard is returned at the entry slot. The SmarTrip target is located on the inside of the faregate for easier access.
- An accessible **TTY-equipped** telephone is located on the **mezzanine** level of each rail station.
- The **Passenger Information Display System** (PIDS) signs are located on each platform and mezzanine of every rail station. These displays can:
  - let customers know when the next trains are **scheduled** to arrive;
  - **alert** customers to service delays;
  - provide information about elevator outages;
  - identify how to make free shuttle arrangements when elevators are out of service.
- Emergency intercoms are located on pylons marked with a white **strip** or the word HELP on the rail platforms. Intercom instructions are in both raised alphabet and Braille.
- All key and new stations feature **bumpy tiles** to alert customers who are blind or have low vision that they are nearing the edge of the platform. (See list of Metro rail stations with bumpy tiles.)
- Flashing lights at the edge of the platforms alert customers that a train is approaching.

Elevators

- Metro operates elevators at all of its rail stations.
- In rail stations, directional signs to elevators are located on the platform information pylons and on wall **mounted** station name signs. They include the International Symbol of Accessibility and an arrow in the direction of the elevator.

Rail Cars

• **Gap reducers** have been installed on all rail cars. They reduce the gap between the platform and the rail car by an additional 1½ inches, making it easier for a wheelchair user or a person with a mobility device to enter and exit the train safely.

• **Barriers** between rail cars alert customers who are blind or have low vision of the space between the rail cars so they do not mistake this space for the door to the inside of the rail car.

• Priority seating for people with disabilities and senior citizens is located in all rail cars **adjacent to** the center doors.

• Emergency **intercoms** are located at both ends of each rail car. Intercom information is in both raised alphabet and Braille, and a call button is accessible for wheelchair users.

Words & Expressions

display /dɪ'spleɪ/ v. 显示；表现；陈列
　　　　 n. 显示；炫耀
dual mode vehicle （DMV）两用车
handicapped /'hændikæpt/ adj. 残疾的；有生
　　　　　　　理缺陷的
　　　　 n. 残疾人
license plate 车辆牌照
pylon /'paɪlən/ n. 指示塔；桥塔；高压线铁塔
contrast /'kɒntrɑːst/ v. 对比，对照
lower panel 下翼片
audio instruction 音频指令
scooter /'skuːtə(r)/ n. 单脚滑行车；小轮摩托车；速可达
TTY-equipped 文字输入设备
mezzanine /'mezəniːn/ adj. 中间的
　　　　　 n. 中层楼；夹楼

Passenger Information Display System 乘客信息显示系统
scheduled /'ʃedjuːld/ adj. 已排程的；预订的
strip /strɪp/ n. 条状
　　　　 v. 脱去衣服；除去
bumpy tile 崎岖不平的瓷砖
mount /maʊnt/ v. 嵌入；安装；爬上
gap reducer 空隙减少装置
barrier /'bæriə(r)/ n. 屏障，障碍物；界线
　　　　 v. 把……关入栅栏
adjacent to 邻近的，毗连的
intercom /'ɪntəkɒm/ n. 对讲机；内部通话装置

M3-10

Question

After reading, can you generalize the accessible facilities for the disabled? What are they?

Chapter Four
Metro Turnstile Entrance and Exit

Learning Outcomes

On completion of the module, you will be able to:

1. Get familiar with the facilities around the turnstile
2. Know how to guide passengers to get through the turnstile
3. Know how to request foreign passengers to do safety inspection
4. Know how to solve problems in case of emergency

Overview of the Module

  This chapter will introduce the metro turnstiles and other facilities. It will help metro staff and passengers get familiar with these facilities. And it will also help metro staff know how to guide passengers to get through turnstiles. At the same time, safety inspection is also required to ride the train. It will help metro staff know how to request passengers to do safety inspection. In case of emergency, it will help metro staff know how to solve some problems.

Unit 1
Turnstiles and Other Facilities

What You Will Learn in This Unit

  1. The use of metro turnstile
  2. Buying a ticket in the ticket center from a ticket machine
  3. Swipe a metro ticket

Part I Getting Started

  The following are the general introduction of metro facilities and turnstiles. Write down their correct English names below.

（1）闸机 _____   （2）刷卡 _____

（3）闸机屏幕 _____   （4）自动售票机 _____

Part II Studying

A. Conversations

Conversation 1

It's Sunday today and the weather is nice. Mary takes Toby out for the day. They will go to Tianfu Square to take some pictures in the morning and then to Ocean Park in the afternoon. They want to take the metro from Tianfu Square to Ocean Park. They are now at Tianfu Square. It's crowded and there are a lot of entrances. Mary doesn't know which way to go. So, she goes to ask a metro staff member.

M4-1

Mary: Toby, wait here, okay? I'll go to ask somebody which way we have to go.

Toby: Okay, Mom.

Mary asks the nearest metro staff.

Mary: Excuse me. Where can I buy a ticket?

SM: Okay, you can buy a ticket in the ticket center or on the ticket machine. If you buy the ticket in the ticket center, you only need to tell them which stop you will get off. Then the metro staff will tell you how much you should pay for it. If you buy the ticket on the ticket machine, you are supposed to input the starting stop and the ending stop, then after you insert the change into the machine, you can get your metro card.

Mary: Okay, thank you so much!

Mary arrives at the ticket center.

Mary: Excuse me, could you please tell me which line I am supposed to take, Line 1 or Line 2? I want to take my son to Ocean Park. Do I have to take Line 1 to get there?

SM: Yes, Madam. You can take Line 1 to Ocean Park. After you buy the ticket, please go through the security check and then go through a turnstile with a green arrow on it. Go down to the platform for Line 1.

Mary: Okay. Thanks.

SM: You're welcome. Have a nice trip.

Conversation 2

Mary doesn't know how to pass through the turnstile, so she turns to a metro staff member for help.

Mary: Excuse me, would you please tell me how I could pass through the turnstile?

SM: Okay, no problem. Did you buy the ticket?

Mary: Yes, I bought the ticket from the ticket center.

SM: Great, please take out your ticket, and I will show you how to swipe the card.

Mary takes out the ticket, waiting for the instructions.

SM: Okay, do you see the turnstile screen? That is where you are supposed to swipe your card. Please tap the ticket on the sensor on your right-hand side until the turnstile opens before proceeding forward.

Mary then taps the ticket on the sensor, and the turnstile opens. She passes through the turnstile.

Mary: Thank you so much!

SM: Please keep the ticket. When you get off the train, you will need to tap the ticket on the sensor again to get out.

Mary: Thanks for reminding me. Otherwise, I may throw away the ticket.

B. Words & Expressions

sensor /ˈsensə(r)/ *n.* 感应器

proceed /prəˈsiːd/ *v.* 前行

tap /tæp/ *v.* 轻敲

remind /rɪˈmaɪnd/ *v.* 提醒

green arrow 绿色箭头

passing error 通行错误

turnstile screen 闸机屏幕

C. Notes

1. 您好，您可以在地铁车站的自动售票机或车站"票务中心"办理充值业务。

    Hello, you may recharge your passcard at the ticket machine or the ticket center.

2. 请右手持卡，刷卡通过闸机。

    Please use your right hand to hold the ticket and swipe it as you pass through the turnstile.

3. 请将卡轻触右侧闸机感应区，待扇形门打开后通过。

    Please tap the ticket on the sensor on your right hand until the turnstile opens before proceeding forward.

4. 乘坐自动扶梯时，请抓好扶手，左行右立，小心安全。

When you are on an escalator, please hold on to the handrail, stand on the right of the escalator and let other passengers pass by your left side. Stay safe.

5. 车票只有当日有效。
    Tickets are only valid on the day of purchase.
6. turnstile：闸门，也称扇形门。这是地铁通行的必经之路。各个城市的闸门稍有不同，有的地铁闸门是刷卡出入，有的地铁闸门是持卡轻触闸机屏幕出入。
7. ticket machine：自动售票机。地铁入口处一般设有自动售票机，乘客可以选择在自动售票机上购票，这样可以节约时间。自动售票机可以用现金或银行卡支付。

Part III Your Turn

A. Discussion

1. If Mary lost Toby when she went to ask the metro staff and she asked you for help, what would you do?
2. If you see a child wandering by himself / herself, what would you do?
3. If someone asks you for help to buy a ticket on the ticket machine, what would you do?

B. Translation

Please translate the following sentences into English.

1. 我们会给你提供一张免费票，你就用这张票出闸吧。
   _____.

2. 您卡里的余额不足，请去售票厅补足费用。
   _____.

3. 请将单程卡插入右边回收口，待扇形门打开，再通行。
   _____.

4. 您的车票是无效票，请到票务中心更新。
   _____.

C. Reading Comprehension

Top 10 Tips for taking the London Underground

The London Underground is one of the best and most **comprehensive** transport networks in the world with around 24 million journeys made each day, so it's important that everything runs smoothly to avoid **delays**.

Check out these top tips to travel by tube like a Londoner and learn what to expect when you arrive.

1. Keep right on the escalator

London Underground asks that you stand on the right when taking the escalator and leaving the left free for others to walk up / down. If you're travelling in a big group, or with lots of shopping bags, stand and stay right and let others pass by—it will speed up the process and be a more pleasant journey for everyone!

2. Remember the "rush hour"

The tube network is very busy during "rush hour" with commuters moving around the city. You can expect the trains and stations to be **overcrowded** between 7:30 and 9:30 in the morning and between 17:00 and 19:00 in the evening.

3. Have your ticket ready at the barrier

Sometimes there can be a bit of a **bottleneck** at ticket barriers, especially before 9:30 a.m. and around 6:00 p.m. during the rush hours. Make sure you have your ticket ready at the barrier so you can move in and out of the station smoothly.

4. Don't panic—you can always go back again

If you've caught the wrong tube or missed your stop—don't panic! London Underground trains run every 2-7 minutes depending on the line so just get off at the next stop and **locate** yourself by a printed tube map on the platform to work out your next step.

5. Move down the platform to find more space

As you enter the station platform you will often find more room if you walk down to the ends of the platform. Here, the train **carriages** are usually the emptiest as well, perfect if you're looking for a place to sit.

6. Let people off the train first

It helps everyone use the busy underground to let people off the tube before you **board** it; allowing more room for you to get on and passengers to alight from the train.

7. Check line closures before you travel

If possible, check ahead and plan your journey to make sure there are no delays or closures on the lines you need to travel—especially at the weekends when **maintenance** work is common. TFL's website provides live network **updates** and will alert you to any **disruptions** and suggest alternative routes in advance.

8. Carry a bottle of water in the warmer months

The London Underground is over 150 years old and although the trains have been **modernized**, many still lack air conditioning and cooling units. Make sure you take a bottle of water with you, especially in the summer, as the long tube journeys can get very hot **at peak times**.

9. Keep your **personal belongings** safe

Like in any large city be wary of **pickpockets** operating in the busy stations and tubes. Carry a bag with **zips** and keep your personal belongings and valuable items with you and safely stored away to avoid any **incidents**.

10. Don't be afraid to ask for help

London Undergrounds **are well staffed with** helpful London Transport officers who can guide you to the nearest exit, or help you plan your **onward journey**. Usually there is one at every main station platform—if not, go up the escalators into the **entrance foyer** where there will be ticket desks, free maps and **information leaflets**.

Words & Expressions

comprehensive /ˌkɒmprɪˈhensɪv/ *adj.* 综合的，广泛的
delay /dɪˈleɪ/ *v.* 耽搁
overcrowded /ˌəʊvəˈkraʊdɪd/ *adj.* 过度拥挤的
bottleneck /ˈbɒtlnek/ *n.* 阻碍，瓶颈；障碍物
locate /ləʊˈkeɪt/ *v.* 找出……的准确位置；确定……的准确地点
carriage /ˈkærɪdʒ/ *n.* 客车厢
board /bɔːd/ *v.* 上船（或火车、飞机、公共汽车等）
maintenance /ˈmeɪntənəns/ *n.* 维护；保养
update /ˌʌpˈdeɪt/ *v.* 更新；校正
disruption /dɪsˈrʌpʃn/ *n.* 妨碍；扰乱

modernize /ˈmɒdənaɪz/ *v.* 使……现代化
at peak time 在高峰时期
personal belongings 个人物品
pickpocket /ˈpɪkˌpɒkɪt/ *n.* 扒手
zip /zɪp/ *n.* 拉链
incident /ˈɪnsɪdənt/ *n.* 事件
be staffed with 配备了……人员
onward journey 续程
entrance foyer 入口门厅
information leaflet 信息传单

M4-4

After reading, write T for True or F for False.

(　　) 1. London Underground asks that you stand on the left when taking the escalators and leaving the left free for others to walk down.

(　　) 2. You can expect the trains and stations to be overcrowded between 7:00 and 9:00 in the morning and between 6:00 and 8:00 in the evening.

(　　) 3. London Underground trains run every 3-8 minutes depending on the line.

(　　) 4. The London Underground is over 150 years old and although the trains have been modernized, many still lack air conditioning and cooling units.

(　　) 5. Carry a bag with zips and keep your personal belongings and valuable items with you and safely stored away to avoid any incidents.

Unit 2
Contraband

What You Will Learn in This Unit

1. Contraband items in metro
2. Consequence of bringing the contraband
3. Other emergency in bringing the contraband

Part I　Getting Started

Please write down the correct English names for the following pictures.

（1）地铁违禁品 _____

（2）易燃物品 _____

（3）易爆物品 _____

（4）危险品 _____

Part II Studying

A. Conversations

Conversation 1

Victor's bag is going through the security machine, and the machine makes the "beep, beep" sound. The metro staff member asks Victor to open his bag.

SM: Excuse me, could you please open your bag?

Victor: What's up?

SM: You have contraband in your bag. Please open your packages for inspection. Please cooperate.

M4-5

Victor: What? I have contraband in my bag? It's impossible.

SM: Did you hear the "beep" sound? The machine tells us there is contraband in your bag. For your and other passengers' safety, please open your bag for inspection.

Victor: Okay, whatever! Go ahead.

SM: Sir, we found a knife in your bag. This item is prohibited within the station premises.

Victor: Well, it is only for cutting fruits.

SM: I'm sorry, but this item is not allowed inside the premises. You may not bring this inside the station, because it's a threat to the safety of other passengers.

Victor: Then what should I do with it?

SM: Please choose another means of transportation or you are welcomed to leave this item here with us and take it once you return from your trip.

Victor: Okay. I would like to leave this item here.

SM: Thanks for your cooperation.

Conversation 2

Then Victor asks a metro staff member about the contraband instructions.

Victor: Excuse me, could you please tell me what the contraband items include?

SM: Okay, the contraband items include flammable explosive items, firearms, ammunitions, controlled knives, poisons and radioactive items. They are forbidden inside the station.

M4-6

Victor: Got it! If someone like me who doesn't know the rules brings the contraband items, how do you deal with it?

SM: Well, our security inspection machine will beep, and we will know some contrabands are in the bag. And then we will ask passengers to take them out. They can leave this item here with us and take it once they return from their trip or they can choose other means of transportation.

Victor: If someone refuses to take it out, what will you do?

SM: In that case, we will call the police to deal with it. For all passengers' safety, we never allow anyone to bring contraband into the station.

Victor: OK. By the way, shall I pay the fine for this?

SM: Since you cooperate well with us, you don't have to pay the fine. You only need to sign here. And then you can come back to get it only if show your ID card.

Victor: Thank you so much! I learned a lot today! I don't think I will bring any contraband any more.

SM: Perfect!

B. Words & Expressions

contraband /ˈkɒntrəbænd/ n. 违禁品
flammable /ˈflæməbl/ adj. 易燃的
explosive /ɪkˈspləʊsɪv/ adj. 易爆炸的
hazardous /ˈhæzədəs/ adj. 有危险的
dimension /daɪˈmenʃn/ n. 尺寸
conceal /kənˈsiːl/ v. 隐藏
recycling /ˌriːˈsaɪklɪŋ/ n. 回收利用
take care of /keep 保管

force through 强行通过
electronic purse 电子钱包
special inspection 特别检查
restricted access 受限访问
security staff 安检人员
security check at the entrance gate 入口处的安检
tickets check at the exit gate 出站口检票

M4-7

C. Notes

1. 您包里有违禁品，请打开包接受检查，请您配合。
You have contraband in your bag. Please open your bag for inspection. Please cooperate.

2. 打扰一下，这是违禁品，按照规定不允许进站上车。
Excuse me, this item is prohibited within the station premises.

3. 打扰一下，这不能带入地铁站，对其他乘客的安全会造成威胁，请您选择其他交通工具。
Excuse me, this item cannot be brought into the metro station because it's a threat to the safety of other passengers. Please choose other transportation.

4. contraband：违禁品。地铁违禁品包括易燃易爆物品、枪支弹药、管制刀具、酒精等。有些城市除了上述常规违禁物品，还有更细致的规定。例如：北京规定白酒也属于地铁违禁品。

5. 超过规格的自行车须折叠在自行车袋里。
Bicycles must be packed in a bike bag and not exceed the required dimensions.
6. 然而，如果车厢拥挤，地铁人员禁止这些物品携带进车厢。
However, staff may not allow these items aboard if the trains are crowded.

Part III   Your Turn

A. Discussion

Work in groups and discuss the following topics.
1. If someone carries a prohibited item in his/her bag, how would you explain and convince him/her to take it out?
2. What items are prohibited or considered as contraband?
3. If you see a passenger carries a prohibited item and insists on taking the metro, what would you do?

B. Reading Practice

Prohibited Items in Metro

1. Beijing

Beijing has updated its list of prohibited items for metro passengers, and has also vowed to enhance security checks by using more advanced equipment. Passengers are now allowed to carry four cigarette lighters at most. Baijiu, or Chinese white **liquor**, is also on the list for the first time. Metro passengers can take no more than 2,000 milliliters of Baijiu, a hugely popular drink in China.

Also new on the list are matches and **floral water** used to avoid **heat-rash** or **deter** mosquitoes. Passengers are not allowed to carry 10 or more boxes of matches (200 or more matchsticks) on a metro train. The list also set more limits on various tools that can be taken onboard, expanding the list of banned items to kitchen knives, cleavers, some knives used in tailoring, and hammers. The deputy director of the Beijing Police Public Traffic Division, says security equipment will be upgraded to enhance accuracy and speed to cope with large numbers of passengers. He says the ban list is stricter than that for train passengers, as the metro operates in a closed space and the number of passengers reaches close to 10 million.

2. City of Yokohama

Items that can be taken on the metro

As well as items such as bags, sticks, and sports equipment, the following items can be taken on the metro for free as personal items, provided that they meet the size requirements described below.

Length	Up to 100 cm (200 cm for sports equipment)
Combined dimensions	Up to 250 cm
Weight	Up to 30 kg
Number of items	Up to 2

Although the following items are normally prohibited, they may be taken on the metro if the following conditions are met.

(1) Bicycles

Bicycles must be packed in a bike bag and not exceed the above dimensions.

(2) Surfboards

Surfboards must be packed in a surfboard bag with the fin removed and not exceed the above dimensions.

(3) Animals. However, dogs, cats, small birds and other small animals may be taken onto the metro if they satisfy the following conditions.

Animals that are contained (in cages or carrier cases).

Animals that weigh less than 20 kg, including the weight of the container.

The head and other parts of the body must not protrude from the case.

(4) Guide dogs accompanying disabled passengers (seeing-eye dogs, service dogs, and hearing assistance dogs) are allowed onto the metro, including large dogs. (Under the condition that they are labeled **in accordance with** the Law Concerning Assistance Dogs for the Disabled.)

However, staff may not allow these items aboard if trains are crowded, etc.

Items not allowed on the metro (prohibited items)

The following items may not be taken onto the metro.

(1) Hazardous items may cause risk to other passengers.

(2) Items that inconvenience other passengers due to uncleanliness or **odor**.

(3) Sling-type carriers are prohibited, even when the animal is completely concealed.

Animals must not be released from their cases when on the metro.

Words & Expressions

liquor /'lɪkə(r)/ n. 烈性酒；含酒精饮料
floral water 花露水
heat-rash n. 【医】痱子，汗疹
deter /dɪ'tɜː(r)/ v. 制止；阻止

in accordance with 符合；依照；和……一致
odor /'əʊdə(r)/ n. 气味，臭味；名声

M4-8

After reading, write T for True and F for False.

(　　) 1. In Beijing, passengers are allowed to carry four cigarette lighters at most.

(　　) 2. Metro passengers can take no more than 2,000 milliliters of Baijiu in Beijing metro station.

(　　) 3. Passengers are not allowed to carry 10 or more boxes of matches (200 or more matchsticks) on a Beijing metro train.

(　　) 4. Bicycles and surfboards are not allowed to be taken in City of Yokohama metro station.

(　　) 5. Animals are allowed to be taken in Yokohama metro station.

Answer the following questions.

1. What items are not allowed aboard if trains are crowded?

2. What items are not allowed on the metro under any circumstances?

Unit 3
Safety Inspection

What You Will Learn in This Unit

1. Instruction of safety inspection
2. Communication with passengers on safety inspection
3. Leading the passengers through safety inspection

Part I Getting Started

The following are the general introduction of metro facilities around the turnstiles. Write their correct English names below.

（1）传送带 _____   （2）巡逻 _____

（3）安全检查 _____   （4）随身携带行李 _____

Part II Studying

A. Conversations

Conversation 1

Mary takes Toby to go through the security check. The person in front of them (Bailey) has a lot of luggage. She walks through the security machine with one of her bags on her back.

M4-9

SM: Hello. This luggage needs to go through the X-ray machine as well.

Bailey: Oh! Sorry. I forgot I have another bag on me. I just have too much luggage with me.

SM: Thank you for your cooperation.

One of Metro staff calls Bailey after one of her bags went through the X-ray machine.

SM: Excuse me, Madam. May I see what's in your bag?

Mary is standing by the security check. She sees that a metro staff member asks Bailey to open her bag. Mary is worried that it could be a safety issue so she asks the staff.

Mary: What's going on? Why does she have to open her bag?

SM: Hello, Madam. There's nothing to worry about. This is part of our regular security check routine.

Bailey: I bought some cooking oil but it's a bit too heavy. And I didn't want to take the bus. The traffic is bad around this time. That's why I'm riding the metro.

SM: I see. Well, cooking oil is one of the prohibited items because it is a flammable fluid. That's why the Chengdu metro doesn't allow any passenger to carry it on board, for everyone's safety.

Bailey: So, what should I do then? It'll take me at least an hour and a half to go home by bus!

SM: Don't worry. I will have to ask you to sign your name and the item you're carrying before boarding the metro.

Toby: Mom, why does she have to sign her name to get on the metro?

Mary: Let's go to ask someone.

Conversation 2

Bailey is carrying too much luggage. When she tries to swipe her ticket, she drops her ticket. Toby, waiting behind her, helps her swipe the ticket. Bailey steps into the turnstile passage but the turnstile alarms "passing error".

M4-10

SM: Please hold your card with your right hand, and swipe it on the turnstile.

Mary: Toby, you are standing on the left side. Move to the right side to swipe the card.

Toby: Oh! Okay.

Bailey: Thank you so much. What's your name?

Toby: My name is Toby. Why do you have so much stuff?

Bailey: I'm moving to a new place, so I have to move a lot of stuff myself. My new home is really close to Century City Station so it's really nice that I can take the metro.

Mary: I don't know if bicycles are allowed on the metro here. I want to buy a small bike for Toby. I heard there's a bicycle park in Huayang and I want to take him there.

There happens to be a metro staff member standing there to answer the question.

SM: Hi, Madam. If it's a small bicycle, you can bring it onto the metro. But you have to put it in a bag.

Toby: Why do you need a bag?

SM: Oh, it's for safety reason, kid.

Bailey: Oh, I see. I think you can buy a small bike for Toby. I think it's small enough.

Mary: I think so, too. But I don't think it's going to be that convenient anyway.

B. Words & Expressions

formulate /'fɔːmjuleɪt/ *v.* 构想出，规划
urban /'ɜːbən/ *adj.* 都市的
rural /'rʊərəl/ *adj.* 乡村的
patrol /pə'trəʊl/ *v.* 巡逻，巡查
luggage /'lʌɡɪdʒ/ *n.* 行李
stuff /stʌf/ *n.* 东西
renew /rɪ'njuː/ *v.* 更新
invalid ticket 无效票

conveyor belt 传送带
safety check /security check 安全检查
safeguard system 安保系统
carry-on luggage/personal luggage 随身行李
regular security check 常规安全检查
cooking oil 食用油

M4-11

C. Notes

1. 这是违禁品，您不能带进站。但是我们可以帮您保管，您回来的时候可以在我们站取回。

I'm sorry but this item is not allowed inside the premises. You may not bring this inside the station. However, you are welcomed to leave this item here with us and take it once you return from your trip.

2. 您的车票是无效票，请到票务中心更新。

Your ticket is invalid; please get a new one at the ticket center.

3. 请您过安检，接受检查。

Please go through the security check.

4. 请在这里签字。

Sign here, please.

5. 地铁安检的原理：是通过X射线对物体进行透视，从而检测出危险物品。安检仪器中X射线剂量较少，只起透视作用，并不会在透视过的物体上残留，因此不用担心安检仪器对物品产生的辐射会影响人体健康。但仍需要注意的是，安检时切不可图一时之快，把手伸入安检机中取包，毕竟射线是在机器内部进行垂直照射的，手伸入内部会受到辐射。因此，正确接受安检，对人的健康是不会有害的。

6. 地铁安检程序

（1）行李物品检查：旅客进入地铁大厅时，首先将行李物品放入X射线安检设备的传送带上，工作人员通过显示器检查。如发现有异物，须由检查人员开包检查。若存在违禁物品，安检人员有权要求旅客转乘其他交通工具或将违禁物品暂存，对公安机关明令禁止的违禁物品可进行查收，并做好相关记录，对拒不服从安检人员管理情节严重者可移交公安机关。

（2）旅客身体检查：旅客通过特设的探测门，进行身体检查。

（3）检测门发出报警声时，需用手持式金属探测器再查，将可能发出报警声的钥匙、打火机等金属物品掏出来，直到检查时不再发出报警声为止。

Part III Your Turn

A. Discussion

1. If you overheard some passengers discussing about safety on the metro and they seem to be unclear about the procedure, what would you do?

2. What should you pay attention to when a passenger enters the security check?
3. Are you able to explain these safety procedures clearly to a passenger?

B. Reading Practice

Security Screening

Security screening is one of the most important concerns for security at public places such as airports, railway stations and others. It is typically used to detect unlawful objects including metal objects, weapons, liquor products and others. Screening includes scanning of people and their luggage to detect any hazardous objects. Security screening is majorly carried at places such as airports, government offices and border terminal points. **Biometric systems** are the most popular techniques used for screening people as it is the most reliable process for **authentication**. Screening systems based on biometrics method include voice scanners, face scanners, **retina** scanners, **iris** scanners and fingerprint scanners. Luggage and other belongings of the people are often screened by using X-ray scanning machines to check for any prohibited objects in the baggage.

Growing need for security measures at public places is the most significant factor driving the security screening market. Government organizations of different nations across the world focus on **stringent** security processes to **curb smuggling** and terrorist activities. The security screening market has witnessed high growth especially after the disastrous terror attacks in the U. S. and India. Furthermore, security screening market is strongly supported by the development in the information and communication technology (ICT) sector. Technological advancements in sensor technology have led to the emergence of non-immersive and contactless detection devices. Such devices have enabled **regulatory** authorities to enforce robust security solutions while decreasing the inconvenience and intrusion of privacy of people. Modern security screening equipment is capable of screening the bones and other internal body parts for **unethical** and unlawful practices. The electronic passport (E-passport) is one of the latest developments for individual authentication. It is based on the biometric features of the passport holder and helps in reducing the instances of fake passports.

Words & Expressions

security screening 安检
biometric system 生物识别系统
authentication /ɔːˌθentɪˈkeɪʃn/ n. 身份验证，认证
retina /ˈretɪnə/ n. 视网膜
iris /ˈaɪrɪs/ n. 虹膜
stringent /ˈstrɪndʒənt/ adj. 严格的，严厉的

curb /kɜːb/ v. 控制，抑制
smuggle /ˈsmʌɡl/ v. 走私，偷运
regulatory /ˈreɡjələtɔːri/ adj. 监管的，具有监管权的
unethical /ʌnˈeθɪkl/ adj. 不道德的

M4-12

After reading, write T for True and F for False.

(   ) 1. Security screening is typically used to detect unlawful objects including metal objects, weapons, liquor products and others.

(   ) 2. Screening includes scanning of people and their luggage to detect any harmful objects.

(   ) 3. The security screening market has witnessed low growth especially after the disastrous terror attacks in the U. S. and India.

(   ) 4. Modern security screening equipment is capable of screening the bones and other internal body parts for ethical and lawful practices.

(   ) 5. Growing need for security measures at private places is the most significant factor driving the security screening market.

Unit 4
Emergency

What You Will Learn in This Unit

1. Some emergency situations in metro station
2. Measures to solve these problems

Part I   Getting Started

Please write down the correct English names for the following pictures.

（1）禁止通行 _____

（2）自动扶梯 _____

（3）地铁盲道 _____

（4）地铁隧道 _____

Part II Studying

A. Conversations

Conversation 1

They are finally at their destination. Mary, Toby, and Bailey get off together. They take the escalator up to the exit. Toby runs over to the turnstile to swipe the ticket for them.

Mary: Toby, this way! Don't you see the sign on the turnstile saying "do not enter"? You have to go through the one with a green arrow.

Toby: Oh, okay. I know it now.

Toby jumps around and runs like the way Mary showed him to the exit. But the turnstile indicates that there's not enough credit on his ticket.

Mary: Toby, what's wrong?

Toby: Mom, I can't get out!

A metro staff member approaches them.

SM: Excuse me, there's not enough credit in your ticket. You will have to go to the ticket center.

Mary: Okay. We're on our way to Ocean Park. Could you tell me which exit I have to go to?

SM: That will be Exit B. After you exit, you can get on Bus 504 A and get off at South Shijiecheng Road Stop.

Mary: Thanks.

M4-13

Conversation 2

Catherine is on her way to South Station. She is waiting in line. Then she saw a thief stealing money from one passenger in front of the waiting line. She is ready to seek help from the metro staff.

Catherine: Hi, Sir. I saw someone stealing from one passenger.

SM: Okay, thanks for telling us this. I will inform our patrols at once. Be calm!

Catherine: I will.

Then the Metro staff member tells this case to a patrol police via intercom. Suddenly some patrol police rush to catch the thief.

SM: Thanks for your help today. Your response is correct. Don't try to catch the thief yourself. First, the thief may carry some dangerous weapons. Second, the crowd may panic, and then some incident may happen. People may push and shove, then someone may get hurt.

Catherine: Yes, I think so. But what should we do if we meet a thief in the train carriage?

SM: A good question! Well, if you meet a thief in the train carriage, you'd better try to text a message to our central control center. The number is ***. Then we will wait for the next stop to catch the thief.

Catherine: Got it. Thank you so much!

SM: Thank you!

M4-14

B. Words & Expressions

escalator /ˈeskəleɪtə/ *n.* 自动扶梯
balance /ˈbæləns/ *n.* 余额
withdraw /wɪðˈdrɔː/ *v.* 取

indicate /ˈɪndɪkeɪt/ *v.* 表明，暗示
emergency /ɪˈmɜːdʒənsɪ/ *n.* 紧急事件
attendant /əˈtendənt/ *n.* 服务人员

M4-15

booth /buːð/ *n.* 售货亭
priority /praɪˈɒrəti/ *n.* 优先权
entitle /ɪnˈtaɪtl/ *v.* 使有资格
outrageous /aʊtˈreɪdʒəs/ *adj.* 粗暴的；无法容忍的
debit card 借记卡
credit card 信用卡

blind walk way 盲道
public transportation system 公共交通系统
seek help 寻求帮助
secondary measure 辅助措施
take...for granted 认为……理所当然

C. Notes

1. Emergency：地铁紧急事件。地铁紧急事件主要包括地震、火灾、偷盗、爆炸以及人员伤害等。
2. 非紧急情况下请不要使用紧急刹车。
Use the emergency brake cord only when the motion of the metro presents an imminent danger to life.
3. 地铁在隧道中时请不要使用紧急刹车。
Do not activate the emergency brake cord, especially in a tunnel.
4. 保持冷静，请不要擅自离开车厢。
Stay calm and don't attempt to leave the train on your own.
5. 紧急情况下，请向地铁工作人员及时汇报。
If there is an emergency, look for a member of the metro crew and report it immediately.
6. 请一定听从现场地铁工作人员、其他交通运输工作人员以及救护人员的指令。
It is important that you follow the instructions of our metro crews, other transit employees, and rescue personnel on the scene.
7. 大部分情况下你只需挪到同车另一节车厢。
In most instances all you need to do is to move to another car on the same train.

Part III　Your Turn

A. Discussion

1. If Toby inserted his Tianfu Card in the machine as he passed the turnstile, what would you do?
2. If a passenger's Tianfu Card expires and he keeps trying to tap the card while the line gets longer and many passengers are getting upset, what would you do?
3. If a foreign passenger asks you for help, will you show him how to get the destination by metro?

B. Oral Practice

地铁通用标识的描述

你怎样向外籍乘客描述如何通过刷卡闸机？

怎样引导外籍乘客通过安检？

C. Reading Practice

Security Review of the NYC Metro System

(1) Summary of Technology

The NYC metro system is considered one of the most comprehensive public transportation systems in the world. Trains run 24 hours a day, 7 days a week with relatively low fares and **a wide breadth of access**. On the average weekday, 5.5 million customers are served. There are 468 operating stations, each of which is generally standardized with the same security system in place around the city.

As part of the so-called "broken windows" policing strategy, there is fairly strict policing for **fare evasion**.

Stations are **outfitted** with:

- Turnstiles, revolving gates or both, operated only by swiping a metrocard with at least $2.50 of fare.
- At least one emergency exit door, which can be opened from the metro side or **explicitly** by an MTA attendant. The doors are alarmed, although this is changing after years of noise complaints.
- Most stations have an attendant in a booth, both to field questions and to watch out for those attempting to bypass security.
- Occasional security booths, frequently with hidden doors.
- Hidden cameras (although public reminders tell that **surveillance** exists).

(2) Intended Security and Privacy Objectives

The highest priority the MTA has is making sure all customers pay for their service. Most of the above security measures are only to serve that purpose, but there are definitely secondary measures for customer comfort/experience. For example, having an attendant makes stations feel safer, and allows a human to more immediately react to security breaches or dangerous situations alike.

Also, the NYC metro system provides a multitude of payment options, including single-ride card, weekly, monthly and automatic refilling cards.

(3) Potential Adversaries, Threats and Weaknesses

- Fare evaders are the most **prominent** threat. There are a **multitude** of physical security exploits that I am aware of, including jumping/ducking the turnstiles and walking through the emergency exit gate when it's been pushed open by someone from the other side.
- Student metrocards given to K-12 NYC public school system students give 3 free rides a week on weekdays, but they are not technically allowed to be used except for going to and from school. Policing for this is **shoddy** at best and it is a difficult policy to enforce.
- Any sort of unlimited metrocard (monthly, weekly, etc.) can be used by multiple people.
- It is fairly easy to fit two average sized people in one turnstile turn to save fare.
- Not all stations have fare card machines, making it difficult for those without cards to pay and encouraging exploitation.

(4) Further Defenses and Suggestions

• Revolving gates are impossible to **circumvent**, as there is no way to jump or duck around them. More similar systems could be implemented. One potential downside is a higher risk for long lines.

• Fines are frequently given to fare evaders upwards of $75.

• Unlimited metrocards enforce a 15-minute waiting period between uses. This reduces the likelihood of a pass-back, without hurting the user's experience much.

• Many of the more crowded stations have hidden police doors from which officers will emerge upon witnessing a violation. I find this concept very strange as if officers were **in plain sight** (as they are frequently as well). The individual would likely have been deterred from attempting to exploit the system.

• Some stations maintain the appearance of security much better than others. That is to say some stations obviously have no attendants, making them appear much more **vulnerable**. Perhaps placing more obvious security cameras in these stations would go a long way toward deterring potential offenders.

(5) Conclusion

The NYC metro system is taken for granted by most of the city's millions of residents. You are raised on the **assumption** that you are entitled to get anywhere else in the city 24/7. While the services the MTA provides are many, they are not free. Compared to many other transit systems, NYC is relatively secure and doesn't sacrifice the user experience all that much to do so. Consider the MBTA, where your ticket is only examined long after the train has left—in New York, you are confronted with payment much earlier in the ride, causing a potential exploiter to weigh the risks of evading fare in the station and providing a **static** series of obstacles rather than a moving ticketing agent who could **theoretically** be **susceptible** to a whole other level of social engineering or even simple evasion.

Interestingly, the MTA estimates it's lost fares at $100,000,000, a figure I believe is a little outrageous given the present security measures. However, this figure includes fare evasions on city buses, which is allegedly much worse than in the metro.

Words & Expressions

a wide breadth of access 大范围的接触
fare evasion 逃票
outfit /ˈaʊtfɪt/ n. 装备；配套设备
explicitly /ɪkˈsplɪsɪtli/ adv. 明确地；明白地
surveillance /sɜːˈveɪləns/ n. （对犯罪嫌疑人或可能发生犯罪的地方的）监视
prominent /ˈprɒmɪnənt/ adj. 重要的，著名的，杰出的
multitude /ˈmʌltɪtjuːd/ n. 众多；大量

shoddy /ˈʃɒdi/ adj. 做工粗糙的；劣质的
circumvent /ˌsɜːkəmˈvent/ v. 设法回避，绕过
in plain sight 一目了然
vulnerable /ˈvʌlnərəbl/ adj. 脆弱的，易受……伤害的
assumption /əˈsʌmpʃn/ n. 假设，假定
static /ˈstætɪk/ adj. 静止的，静态的

theoretically /ˌθɪəˈretɪkli/ *adv.* 从理论上说，照理说

susceptible /səˈseptəbl/ *adj.* 易受影响的，敏感的

After reading, write T for True and F for False.

(　　) 1. Stations are outfitted with at least one emergency exit door.

(　　) 2. The highest priority the MTA has is making sure all customers pay for their service.

(　　) 3. All stations have fare card machines.

(　　) 4. Fines are frequently given to fare evaders upwards of $70.

(　　) 5. Unlimited metrocards enforce a 10-minute waiting period between uses.

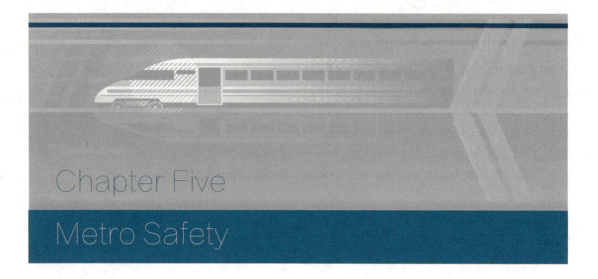

Chapter Five
Metro Safety

Learning Outcomes

On completion of the module, you will be able to:
1. Know the general information of metro safety service
2. Explain the safety requirement to passengers
3. Solve problems in case of urgent situation

Overview of the Module

  Safety is of the highest priority in the whole metro system. Metro brings urban people great convenience in commute and reduces the congestions of public bus system in cities; however, it also presents some potential safety issues, such as fire, pushing, stampede, explosion, etc. Since safety is the top consideration in riding the metro, this chapter aims at safety considerations related to the operation of metro and the safety of passengers.

Unit 1
Metro Exterior Safety

What You Will Learn in This Unit

1. Patrolling
2. Facilities check
3. Some basic safety procedures

Part I Getting Started

Please write down the correct English names for the following pictures.

（1）扶梯 _____　　（2）紧急电话 _____

Part II　Studying

A. Conversations

Conversation 1

There's an announcement about the safety awareness campaign by the Beijing Metro. Many and Jack take Toby to join the event. First they will learn the basic safety procedures.

SM: Hello, everyone. Thank you for joining us today to take part in the Beijing Metro's safety awareness campaign. First, let's start with learning all the basic safety procedures and some other basic things you should always keep in mind.

Andy: Fire and dangerous goods.

SM: Right. So, what do you have to do when there's a fire?

Toby: Run as fast as you can!

SM: Haha, good one, kid. Well, when there's a fire, it's best to stay calm and you shouldn't run.

Toby: Ohh.

SM: The second thing is to wait for the instructions from the metro staff and follow the safety procedure. If an evacuation is needed, strictly follow the instructions.

Jack: I think the metro's facility is pretty safe. I don't think there would be such a case.

SM: Right, but it's better to know what to do just in case such an unlikely emergency ever occurs. It's also good for metro riders to know some basic information regarding our facilities in case there's an emergency.

Andy: Well, that's a good idea. Since I'll be taking Toby on the metro more often, it'll be good if he knows a bit more about the metro. You never know when such an emergency will ever happen. What are other kinds of emergencies that may occur while riding a metro then?

SM: That's true.

M5-1

Conversation 2

Then the Metro staff member introduces the following emergency situations.

SM: Well, you mentioned dangerous items earlier. As a passenger, what would you do when you find out there's a dangerous item near you?

M5-2

Chapter Five　Metro Safety　▶▶ *073*

Toby: I know! Go to the police! Call 110!

Jack: Toby, I think if you find something strange, it's best to stay away from it.

SM: If there's a flammable item or any dangerous item, don't touch it. Stay away from them and report it to metro staff. Now, what if there's a gas leak? What should you do?

Andy: What? Is that possible? That's too dangerous.

SM: Haha, this is safety awareness training. We have to think about all the possibilities. Of course, a gas leak would be a really rare case here in Chengdu. I don't think it would happen actually.

Andy: I think so, too. But let's say if there were a gas leak? what should we do?

SM: When there's a gas leak, the first thing to keep in mind is to remain calm and don't panic. Listen carefully for any announcement or instruction from metro staff. Use your hands or any clothing to cover your mouth and nose. Follow the directed route for evacuation and stay away from the source of the gas leak.

Jack: Oh! I just thought of another scenario. What about if someone falls down into the train track?

Andy: Yeah, what would happen?

SM: When you see someone fall off from the platform, you shout out loud to get metro staff's attention immediately. Our staff will temporarily cut down the electricity to prevent that passenger from being electrified before getting him or her back up to the platform.

Andy: Wow, I learned quite a lot today.

Jack: Me, too. There are so many things we never thought about. I don't think I would have known what to do if such an incident ever happened. Now that I know it, I think I'll be less scared.

SM: There's no need to be scared when an unlikely event occurs in a metro line. What is scary is those unlikely events that you don't know how to react to. The best thing is not to panic. Get yourself familiar with possible emergency events and learn what to do in those cases. This way you will be able to reach a safe place.

B. Words & Expressions

announcement /əˈnaʊnsmənt/ n. 通告；预告
campaign /kæmˈpeɪn/ n. 运动；战役；竞选活动
procedure /prəˈsiːdʒə(r)/ n. 程序
evacuation /ɪˌvækjuˈeɪʃn/ n. 疏散
facility /fəˈsɪləti/ n. 设施；设备
occur /əˈkɜː(r)/ v. 发生
regarding /rɪˈɡɑːdɪŋ/ prep. 关于
panic /ˈpænɪk/ n. 恐慌 v. 使惊慌
source /sɔːs/ n. 源头
scenario /səˈnɑːrɪəʊ/ n. 设想；方案
temporarily /ˈtemprərɪli/ adv. 暂时地

electrify /ɪˈlektrɪfaɪ/ v. 使……触电
safety awareness 安全意识
keep in mind 牢记
train track 火车轨道
cut down 减少；裁减
compressed gas 压缩气体
gas leak 煤气泄漏
pets and livestock 宠物及禽畜
non-public area 非公共区域
liquefied gas 液化气体
flammable liquid/solid 易燃液体/固体

M5-3

C. Notes

1. 禁止携带长度超过1.8米、高度超过1.6米、重量超过30千克的物品进站。

Any item that is longer than 1.8 meters, taller than 1.6 meters, and heavier than 30 kilograms is prohibited to be carried on board.

2. 禁止携带折叠自行车进站。

Folding bicycles are prohibited within the station premises.

3. 禁止携带充气气球进站。

Inflatable balloons are prohibited within the station premises.

4. 禁止携带铁制品进站。

Any item that is made of iron is prohibited within the station premises.

5. 禁止携带自行车、电动车、平板车进站。

Bicycles, electrical scooters and platform trolleys are prohibited within the station premises.

6. 禁止携带易燃易爆、有毒、腐蚀、放射性等危险品进站。

Inflammable items, explosives in any form, poisons, corrosives, radioactives, and any dangerous goods are strictly prohibited within the station premises.

7. 禁止携带枪支弹药和尖锐物品进站。

Any type of firearm, ammunition, or sharp object is strictly prohibited within the station premises.

Part III Your Turn

A. Speaking Practice

Describe the meanings of the metro signs.

_____ _____ _____ _____

_____

In what situations do we need to use emergency alarm?

B. Discussion

1. If you were asked to provide safety training, how would you conduct it?

2. If you were asked by a foreign passenger regarding how to use safety equipment, how would you explain it?

C. Reading Practice

Riding the New York Metro

The metro is a fast, **affordable** way to get around New York City. Read these tips for riding the New York City Metro and you'll be traveling around like a local New Yorker in no time.

1. Finding Metro Entrances

Entrances are typically located on street corners with a staircase for **descending** into the station. If a station is marked with a large green ball, you can buy a MetroCard inside; if a station is marked with a red ball, you need to already have a MetroCard to enter.

2. How Free Transfers Work

A MetroCard allows one free transfer within 2 hours of swiping your card. You can transfer from bus to metro, metro to bus, bus to bus, or between select metro stations. (Free metro to metro transfers only apply when you are required to exit the station to make your connection.) If you take the metro one way and the bus back, you can get two rides for one fare, but you can't transfer between buses going in opposite directions (e.g. Madison and Fifth Avenue buses).

3. Maps in Metro Stations

One of the most helpful things about New York City's metro stations is the map located near the entrances. In addition to having a map of the metro system, there is normally a neighborhood map that shows the streets in the area in detail. It's a good idea to check out the map before you leave the metro, but it's also great to know that if you're lost near a metro station, you can always duck in and check out a map to find your way around.

4. Check the Sign Before You Swipe

At many Metro stations, there are separate entrances for trains running uptown and downtown. Once you swipe your card, you can't get a refund, so be sure to check the sign to make sure you're swiping your card at the right entrance. You can also ask an attendant for help if you're confused about where to enter.

5. Hold on

If you don't get a seat, make sure you find a pole to hold when the train begins to move—it is difficult to keep steady without holding on when the metro starts and stops, as it is not always as smooth a ride as you might hope. And no one likes it when you fall on him or her because you weren't holding on.

6. Don't Lean on the Poles

Just because you're tired, it doesn't mean it's all right to lean up against a pole in the metro car. When someone leans on the poles, it makes difficult for other folks to hold on when the train is moving.

7. Keep Your Bags (and Your Feet) Off the Seats

Keep in mind that even if the metro isn't very crowded when you board, it may get more crowded quickly, so you should keep your bags on your lap or on the floor in front of you if you're sitting down. Keeping your feet off the seat ensures that other folks have a clean place to sit when they ride the metro.

8. Move to the Center of the Car

When trains are crowded, it is important to move to the center of the metro car to make room for other riders. Standing by the door even if you move to the side makes it difficult for people getting on and off the train.

9. In an Emergency Stay in the Metro Car

The safest place is inside the metro car. In the event of a situation where you have to leave the metro car, you should know about blue and white lights in the metro car. Blue lights in the metro mark the spot where there is a telephone, power off switch, and fire extinguisher. Pick up the phone after switching off the power—otherwise, power will be restored after about a minute. Five white lights in a circle or on a bar mark an exit to the street.

Words & Expressions

affordable /əˈfɔːdəbl/ *adj.* 买得起的；价格合理的；负担得起的

descend /dɪˈsend/ *v.* 下来；下去；下降

M5-4

After reading, write T for True and F for False.

(　　) 1. If a station is marked with a large red ball, you can buy a MetroCard inside.

(　　) 2. A MetroCard allows one free transfer within 1 hour of swiping your card.

(　　) 3. Blue lights in the metro mark the spot where there is a telephone, power off switch, and fire extinguisher.

(　　) 4. Five blue lights in a circle or on a bar mark an exit to the street.

(　　) 5. When trains are crowded, it is important to move to the center of the metro car to make room for other riders.

Unit 2
Station Interior Safety

What You Will Learn in This Unit

1. Passengers riding safety instruction
2. Station interior safety facilities

Part I Getting Started

Please write down the correct English names for the following pictures.

（1）地铁栏杆 _____   （2）安全检查 _____

Part II Studying

A. Conversations

Conversation 1

After the training, Andy and Jack take Toby to the new exhibition center. Toby is excited and runs off ahead. A metro staff member comes over…

M5-5

SM: Excuse me, is he with you?

Andy: Yes, this is my nephew. What happened?

SM: Please tell him not to run in the station. It's for safety reasons.

Andy: Oh, okay. Toby, come over here. You can't run around like this in the metro station. Weren't we just in the safety awareness training? Did you already forget everything that the metro staff told us?

Toby: Fine.

After boarding the train, they see a baby is urinating inside the train.

Toby: Hey, Andy, look! That baby is peeing inside the train!

Andy: Ah, Toby! There's no need to shout it out loud like this. I can see it. I don't think that should be allowed here.

Toby: I want to pee in here, too!

Andy: Come on, Toby. We'll get off soon.

Toby walks up to the man who is holding the baby who was urinating.
Toby: Hey, Sir. You can't pee in here.
The man laughs awkwardly.
Man: Kid, you're right, but we have to go all the way to the last station of the metro line. This baby can't wait.
Andy: Well, you can just get off at one of the stations to go to use the restroom. I don't think it's good to just let the baby urinate in here.
The man turns a bit embarrassed.
Man: Right, I should have thought of that. Sorry about this.

Conversation 2

Toby sees a box with a fire extinguisher inside the metro and asks Andy what it is and how to use it. But Andy and Jack don't know how to use it. After getting off the train, they ask a metro staff member.

Andy: Hello, excuse me. We were on the train and we saw a fire extinguisher. But we don't know how to use it. Could you tell us?
SM: No problem. In every car of the metro, there are two fire extinguishers. In case of a fire, pull the two black handles down to open the box and get to the fire extinguisher.
Jack: I also saw a sign for an emergency door. Is there any other thing we need to know in case there's an emergency? Can you tell us a bit more?
SM: Of course. There's a handle to open an emergency door in every car. Just pull the handle bar down to about 90 degrees to open the door. Once the train comes to a complete stop, use both hands to open up the doors at the platform.
Jack: Oh, this seems really complicated!
SM: Oh, and when you're opening up the emergency doors, you need to tell other passengers to stay calm and do not push to get out. If not, the door will not open.
Andy: What's this emergency button for?
SM: In case a passenger needs to contact metro staff for assistance or report an emergency, he or she can press this button and hold it. This red emergency button is used when you need to open the doors during an emergency. So, if you want to use it, lift up the plastic cover and then press the red button. You will be directed to talk to the operator immediately.
Andy: What if there's a need for an evacuation, what should we do then?
SM: Well, in that case, you can use the access door and evacuation ladder. There are doors leading to both ends of the train. To open the emergency doors, pull down the red handle at the top of the door. Then, push the door to get into the operator's cabin. And then, to unlock the evacuation door, use both hands to pull down the red handle at the door. Push the door forward to exit the train.
Andy: Thanks.
SM: My pleasure. If there's anything you don't understand, just ask one of the metro staff. We'll be happy to assist you.

B. Words & Expressions

exhibition /ˌeksɪˈbɪʃn/ *n.* 展览，陈列
awkward /ˈɔːkwəd/ *adj.* 令人尴尬的
embarrass /ɪmˈbærəs/ *v.* 使……窘迫
handle /ˈhændl/ *n.* 手柄 *v.* 操作，处理
plastic /ˈplæstɪk/ *adj.* 塑料的
cabin /ˈkæbɪn/ *n.* 车厢
assist /əˈsɪst/ *v.* 帮助
slippery /ˈslɪpəri/ *adj.* 湿滑的
detonator /ˈdetəneɪtə(r)/ *n.* 雷管
poison /ˈpɔɪzn/ *n.* 毒品
explosive /ɪkˈspləʊsɪv/ *n.* 炸药
firework /ˈfaɪəwɜːk/ *n.* 烟花
corrosion /kəˈrəʊʒn/ *n.* 腐蚀品
smoking /ˈsməʊkɪŋ/ *n.* 吸烟
firecracker /ˈfaɪəkrækə(r)/ *n.* 鞭炮
prank /præŋk/ *v.* 打闹

fire extinguisher 灭火器
station broadcast/announcement 车站通告、广播
flammable and explosive 易燃易爆
strong oxidizing agent 强氧化剂
exit before boarding 先下后上
hand grenade 手榴弹
infectious substance 感染性物品
give a seat 让座
security line 安全线
radioactive substance 放射性物品
safety and emergency facility 安全及紧急设施
personal safety 人身安全
blasting fuse 导火线
shield door 屏蔽门

M5-7

C. Notes

1. 站内禁止吸烟。
Smoking is prohibited within the station premises.
2. 请不要在车站、车厢内或站台上奔跑。
Please do not run in stations or trains or on platforms.
3. 小心地滑，请避开车站内地面湿滑地带。
Wet floors can be slippery, please avoid any wet area in the station.
4. 乘坐扶梯，请拉好扶手。
Use handrails at all times when taking escalators.
5. 请站在站台黄线之外，直到车停稳再靠近车厢。
Please stay behind the yellow line. Do not approach the train until it comes to a complete stop in the station.

Part III Your Turn

A. Discussion

1. If you find an adult holding a child in his arm and helping him urinate inside the metro, what would you do?
2. In case of a fire, do you know how to use the fire extinguisher?

B. Reading Practice

General Safety in Riding the Train

AT THE STATION

When entering stations, you need to watch your steps on stairs and escalators. Hold onto handrails and keep your eyes on the stairs and escalators.

At stations, do not cross the tracks, walk on the trackways or touch the electric third rail.

Do not run in stations, trains or on platforms.

Wet floors can be slippery. Avoid any wet areas in the station if possible. If a wet area is not marked off, report its location to the Station Agent.

Although stairs are constructed with **anti-slip** material, be careful to avoid any water or **debris** that may be on them. Use handrails at all times.

Roller skating, roller blading, bicycle riding and skateboarding are not allowed in stations or on trains. Be aware of passengers' carrying bikes.

For security reasons, make sure you know where your luggage and personal possessions are at all times.

Gasoline, flammable or **volatile solvents**, acids, etc. are not allowed in stations or on trains.

ON THE ESCALATOR

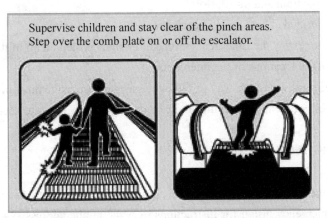

Supervise children and stay clear of the pinch areas. Step over the comb plate on or off the escalator.

Safe use of escalators requires observing the following critical rules. Please Pay Attention:

• Look at the direction of the escalator before you take the first step.

• On escalators, be alert and ready to step off the **tread** when you have reached the landing.

• Keep your feet away from the side of the tread where a shoe may be caught between the tread and the side of the escalator.

Use the Handrail:

• Always use the handrails to maintain your balance.

• Never ride on the handrail. Exit promptly.

Please Don't Use the Escalator if...

• You have limited physical abilities or are carrying large packages and luggage.

• You are carrying a small child in your arms or in a stroller.

• You are carrying or riding a bicycle. Bicycles are not allowed on escalators.

In all of the above instances, we recommend you not to use the escalators.

ON THE PLATFORM

• Please stay behind the yellow and black platform edge **detection tiles**. Do not approach the train until it comes to a complete stop in the station.

• Never sit on the platform edge or touch the outside of the trains!

• Do not cross the tracks or enter the trackway under any circumstances!

• If you drop something on the trackway, do not attempt to retrieve it! Contact the Station Agent for help.

• There is a refuge area underneath the train platform that may provide some protection in the event of an accidental fall onto the track.

• Watch your step when boarding and the narrow gap between the platform edge and the train.

• Stand in the center of the platform and in well-lighted areas.

ON THE TRAIN

• Do not lean against the doors when inside the train.

• Flammable liquids are not allowed in stations or on trains.

• When entering and exiting the train, be sure to watch your step. There is a gap of approximately three inches between the train and the platform.

• Intercoms are located at both ends of each car.

• Take time out to review the Emergency Procedures signs posted on all of the trains.

• Make a note of the locations of the intercoms.

• Please keep luggage out of the way of fellow passengers. Luggage must never block walkways and doorways. To help prevent **tampering**, theft or damage, keep luggage secure and within your sight.

USING EMERGENCY EQUIPMENT

FIRE EXTINGUISHERS

• Emergency fire extinguishers are located on all levels of the stations and are well marked. In the event of an emergency, listen for instructions over the public address system or directly from BART personnel.

• Emergency fire extinguishers are located at the end door of all BART cars. Follow the operating instructions listed on the label.

End Door

INTERCOM

• Locate the intercom on your train.

• Press, and then release, the "Attendant Call" button to speak directly with the Train Operator.

• Use the intercom to ask the Train Operator questions or to report anything you believe is important.

• The Train Operator can contact the BART Control Center to provide whatever or other services are needed.

• If something is happening in the car you are in and you

don't want to be seen calling the Train Operator, walk to the next car and call from there.

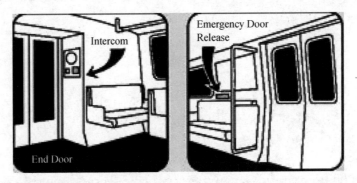

Words & Expressions

anti-slip 防滑

debris /de'briː/ *n.* 残骸；碎片；破片；残渣；垃圾；废弃物

volatile /'vɒlətaɪl/ *adj.* 易变的；无定性的；无常性的；易挥发的

solvent /'sɒlvənt/ *n.* 溶剂；溶媒

tread /tred/ *v.* 踩；踏；践踏；踩碎；行走；步行；走 *n.* 踏；踩；(楼梯的)踏板

detection /dɪ'tekʃn/ *n.* 侦查；探测；察觉；发现

tile /taɪl/ *n.* (贴墙或铺地用的)瓷砖，地砖

tamper /'tæmpə(r)/ *v.* 干预；篡改

After reading, write T for True and F for False.

(   ) 1. Please stay behind the yellow and black platform edge detection tiles. Do not approach the train until it comes to a complete stop in the station.

(   ) 2. Flammable liquids are allowed in stations or on trains.

(   ) 3. When evacuating a train in a metro, only the Train Operator can open the doors.

(   ) 4. Emergency phones located in the tunnel and metro areas are marked with a red light.

(   ) 5. Each car is equipped with two fire extinguishers located next to the doors connecting the cars.

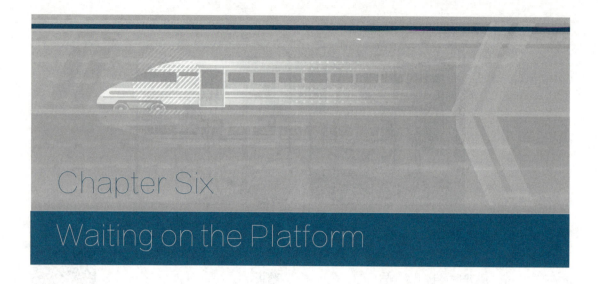

Chapter Six
Waiting on the Platform

Learning Outcomes

On completion of the module, you will be able to:
1. Know how to politely reply to passengers' questions about the train schedule
2. Get to know how to enhance the management of the metro platform
3. Get familiar with facilities on the platform

Overview of the Module

The train schedule is very important in riding the train. Compared with ground transportation system, the underground system is known for its accuracy and high-speed. Therefore, the train schedule becomes especially important for passengers. In this way, this chapter will first help metro staff to explain the train schedule to riders, and also it provides cases about how to explain the delay of train to passengers. Moreover, getting on and off the train is also metro staff's consideration, especially in rush hours. In some cases, train riders will push and shove or stand in front of the yellow line or lean against the platform screen doors. Therefore, this chapter also provides metro staff how to help passengers safely ride the train.

Unit 1
Metro Schedule

What You Will Learn in This Unit

1. Introduction of train schedule
2. Announcement of train delay

Part I Getting Started

1. The following are the general introduction of metro platform facilities and activities. Describe them in English.

（1）站台 _____   （2）排队 _____

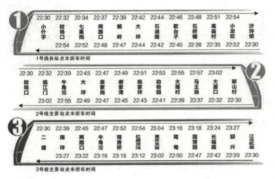

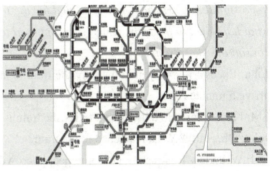

（3）时刻表 _____   （4）地铁线 _____

2. Discuss with your partner about what other facilities you can find in the metro platform.

Part II Studying

A. Conversations

Conversation 1

Kim is going for an interview during the rush hour. He is trying to get in the train and the doors are closing.

SM: Sir, I need you to step out and wait for the next train to arrive. The train needs to depart.

Kim: Ahhhh! I'm running late! Whatever!

SM: Thank you, Sir.

Kim: When's the next one going to be here? Why are there so many people?

SM: It's the rush hour.

Kim: What are rush hours here? 7:00 to 9:00?

M6-1

SM: Pretty much. We schedule rush hours from 7:30 to 9:30 in the morning.

Kim: So, when is the first train in the morning then?

SM: The first Line 1 train leaves Shengxian Lake for Century City at 6:30.

Kim: I wonder how long it takes from Tianfu Square to Tongzilin. Do you know?

SM: It takes about 15 minutes.

Kim: When will the next one get here?

SM: It'll be here in a couple of more minutes. You may look at the announcement screen on the top to see when the next train will arrive.

Kim: I see. Well, I got three more minutes. That's not too bad. Is there a restroom down here?

SM: I'm sorry, but all the washrooms are located before the turnstiles. You will have to go back up.

Kim: Forget it. I'll just wait. Thanks.

SM: Have a safe ride.

Conversation 2

John is waiting at the platform of Xidan Station. He wants to go to Tian'anmen Square to go sightseeing. He has already waited for the train for 15 minutes. He is wondering what happened to the train, which was supposed to arrive 5 minutes earlier. He tries to consult the Metro staff.

M6-2

John: Excuse me, do you know why the train is late today? I think it was supposed to arrive 5 minutes ago.

SM: I am so sorry to tell you that today the train is 10 minutes late.

John: Oh, really? What happened to the train?

SM: Well, now it is rush hour. Some people crowded into the train, and then the door couldn't close. As a result, the train couldn't start at the scheduled time.

John: Okay. Is there anyone hurt?

SM: Fortunately, no one got hurt. And the train got started again.

John: Thank goodness! No one got hurt. Safety is the top priority for riding the train.

SM: Yeah, you are right. Are you in a hurry?

John: Actually, I am from Shanghai. I just want to go to Tian'anmen Square to go sightseeing. I am not in a rush. Therefore, for me I am OK for the delay.

SM: That's better! However, since you are travelling in Beijing, I would like to remind you that you'd better avoid the rush hours that are from 7:30 to 9:30 in the morning and 5:00 to 7:00 in the afternoon. In this way, you can ride the train more comfortably.

John: Thanks for your advice.

Announcement: Ladies and gentlemen, I am so sorry to tell you that Line 1 will be 10 minutes delayed due to some urgent situation. We are so sorry for the inconvenience. Thanks for your understanding.

SM: See, here is the announcement. Hope the passengers will be on time for their work. For our metro staff, safety is more important than accuracy in some cases.

John: That's true! By the way, do you know how I can get to Temple of Heaven if I take the train from Tian'anmen Square?

SM: Yeah, if you are in Tian'anmen Square, you can take Line 1 to transfer in Dongdan Station, and then transfer to Line 5 to Temple of Heaven. The whole ride is about 20 minutes.

John: Thank you so much! So nice talking to you!

SM: Me too, hope you have a safe and pleasant trip in Beijing.

B. Words & Expressions

arrival /əˈraɪvl/ n. 到达；到来
depart /dɪˈpɑːt/ v. 出发
departure /dɪˈpɑːtʃə(r)/ n. 出发
bathroom/restroom/washroom/toilet n. 洗手间
patience /ˈpeɪʃns/ n. 耐心
non-rush hour /off-peak hour 平时
trainline /ˈtreɪnˈlaɪn/ n. 地铁线

interview /ˈɪntəvjuː/ n. 采访
/ˈɪntəˈvjuː/ v. 采访
avoid /əˈvɔɪd/ v. 避免
inconvenience /ˌɪnkənˈviːnɪəns/ n. 不方便；麻烦
accuracy /ˈækjurəsi/ n. 精确

M6-3

C. Notes

1. 在站台

请站在黄线后等待。

等车期间请排队站好。

At the platform:

Please wait behind the yellow line.

Please stand in line while waiting for the train to arrive.

2. 电梯在哪儿？

回答：电梯在这儿\那儿\往这儿走。

乘坐电梯时请抓好扶手，靠右站稳，注意安全。

不要随地乱扔垃圾。

Where is the escalator?

Answer: The escalator is here/over there/this way.

Please hold the handrail when you're on the escalator. Stand on the right. Be safe.

No littering.

3. 询问列车

您好，请问下趟车什么时候到？

请问下趟车还要多久才来？

回答：下趟车几分钟之后到达。

Asking about the train:

Excuse me, when will the next train arrive?

How long will it take for the next train to arrive?

Answer: The next train will arrive in a few minutes.

4. 门会开多久?
回答：大约30秒。
How long do the doors stay open?
Answer: About 30 seconds.

Part III Your Turn

A. Discussion

1. Where is Kim going?
2. Why is Kim upset?
3. Do you know what time the rush hour is in the evening?
4. Do you know how long it takes to travel from Shengxian Lake to Century City?
5. Will you be able to tell Kim how to go to the washroom if asked? Can you instruct him clearly?
6. What kind of information does the announcement screen usually display?

B. Oral Practice

What are these called? Do you know where they are?
这些标志是什么含义？一般在哪里能看到？

C. Reading Comprehension

Idioms about train

Gravy train

Meaning: a position in which a person or group receives excessive and unjustified money or advantages with little or no effort

For example: The top executives were on the gravy train with their huge bonuses.

To get on the gravy train

Meaning: to attempt to make money quickly, easily, and often dishonestly

For example: I wouldn't trust him if I were you, he is always trying to get on the gravy train.

To ride the gravy train

Meaning: to live in ease or luxury

For example: If I had a million dollars, I am sure I could ride the gravy train.

Go off the rails

Meaning: to start behaving in a way that is not generally acceptable, especially dishonestly or illegally

For example: Prince Harry has really gone off the rails recently.

Train of thought

Meaning: the connections that link the various parts of an event or argument together

For example: He was trying to explain how the budget would help to end the recession, but I couldn't follow his train of thought.

Jokes:

Q: Why did the man throw his watch out of the window?

A: He wanted to see time fly.

Q: What's the difference between a TEACHER and a CONDUCTOR?

A: A teacher TRAINS the MIND and a conductor MINDS the TRAIN.

Q: What do you call a person who speaks three languages?

A: Tri-Lingual.

Q: What do you call a person who speaks two languages?

A: Bi-Lingual.

Q: What do you call a person who speaks one language?

A: An American!

Unit 2
Getting On and Off the Train

What You Will Learn in This Unit

1. Get on the train
2. Get off the train

Part I Getting Started

Please write the right English names for the following pictures.

(1) 站台屏蔽门 _____ (2) 地铁闸机 _____

(3) 上车 _____ (4) 下车 _____

Part II Studying

A. Conversations

Conversation 1

Nick and his friend are waiting at Tongji University Station. They are going to Shanghai Train Station to pick up their friends from Beijing. They will first take Line 10 to Nanjing East Road, and then transfer to Line 2 to get to the People's Square, and then take Line 1 to get to Shanghai Train Station.

M6-4

Nick: Excuse me, we are taking Line 10 to Nanjing East Road, do you know how long it will take for the next train to arrive?

SM: Okay. Let me check. Look at the screen above you, which says that the next train will arrive in 5 minutes.

Nick: Okay, thank you so much! Well, since we are freshmen in Tongji University, this is our first time riding the train in Shanghai. Could you please tell me some basic rules of riding the train?

SM: Okay. Welcome to the Shanghai Metro. I would like to tell you some basic rules to ride the train. When you board the train, please wait behind the yellow line, and mind the gap between the train and the platform. Please do not lean against the platform screen doors. During rush hour, please do not push. When the train is full, please wait for the next train. Last but not least, we follow the principle "give way to arrivals before getting on the train".

Nick: Thanks again.

SM: You are very welcome! Where are you going?

Nick: We are getting to the Shanghai Train Station to pick up our friends from Beijing. Do you know how to get there?

SM: Yeah! First you take Line 10 to Nanjing East Road, and then transfer to Line 2 to get off at the People's Square Stop, and then take Line 1 to get to Shanghai Train Station. You don't need to get out of the platform. You can always wait at the platform to take the train. By the way, when you ride the train, please pay attention to the right direction of the train. Moreover, you can check the time from the screen above your head. There is a screen at each platform.

Nick: You are so nice! Thanks a lot!

SM: No problem! Have a safe ride!

Nick: Thanks! Have a nice day!

Conversation 2

Nick and his friend arrive in Shanghai Station. They are asking one of the Metro Staff how to get out of the platform to get to Shanghai Train Station.

M6-5

Nick: Excuse me, Sir. Could you please tell me how we can get out of the platform to get to the Shanghai Train Station?

SM: Okay, no problem. Do you see the escalator on your right-hand side? You can take the escalator to the second floor. And then follow the sign to reach the train station.

Nick: Thanks. Is there an elevator nearby?

SM: Yes, there is. You can go straight about 100 meters on the left, and then you will see the elevator just on your left. However, I think it's faster to take the escalator since there may be a lot of people waiting for the elevator.

Nick: Thanks for your advice. You know, we are going to pick up our friends from Beijing. They have their luggage with them. We think it's more convenient to use the elevator after we pick them up.

SM: Yes. After you pick up your friends, you can use the elevator to go back to the metro station.

Nick: Thank you so much! Have a good day!

SM: You are welcome! Have a good day!

B. Words & Expressions

available /ə'veɪləbl/ *adj.* 可获得的；可利用的
drugstore /drʌg,stɔː/ *n.* 药房；<美>杂货店
portable /'pɔːtəbl/ *adj.* 可携带的

principle /'prɪnsəpl/ *n.* 原则；准则
conductor /kən'dʌktə/ *n.* 售票员
consult /kən'sʌlt/ *v.* 咨询；商议

M6-6

C. Notes

1. 第一趟车什么时候到达？

第一趟车 _____ 分钟后到达 _____ 站。

When will the first train arrive?

Answer: The first train will arrive at _____ Station in _____ minutes.

2. 末班车什么时候到达 _____ 站?

末班车 _____ 点到达 _____ 站。

When will the last train get to _____ Station?

Answer: The last train to _____ Station will be at _____.

3. 地铁运营到什么时候?

晚上10:30左右。

How late does the metro run?

Answer: Until around 10:30 at night.

Part III   Your Turn

A. Speaking Practice

1. Situation: You are one of the metro staff, and you are asked by a foreigner about the train schedule information.

Guest	Staff
咨询对方如何到达飞机场	告诉对方转乘路线、上车注意事项
询问地铁时刻表	告诉对方如何看地铁时刻表以及时刻表的具体位置
询问地铁晚点原因	告诉对方地铁具体晚点原因以及应对措施

2. Discussion

Work in groups and discuss the following topics:

(1) As a metro staff member, how can you explain the train schedule to passengers?

(2) In case of delay of train, how can a metro staff member explain the reason to passengers?

(3) If you meet some passengers standing in front of the yellow line or push around to get on or get off the train, how can you warn them in a polite way?

B. Translation

1. 上车。
2. 请不要靠着门。
3. 请注意列车和站台之间的间隙。
4. 请不要推挤。
5. 列车已满员。
6. 请等待下趟列车。

C. Reading Practice

Read the following passage and decide the statements are true (T) or false (F).

How to Ride the NYC Metro

The metro is the most **frugal** way to travel across New York City. It has 26 train lines—more than any metro system in the world, and while it might be **nerve-wracking** and confusing at first, you'll be a metro pro in no time by learning to read the map, understanding the difference between uptown and downtown and determining the safest place to get on the train. You'll also save money on cab fare and beat the traffic to your destination.

Step 1:

Obtain a metro map to keep with you at all times. Metro maps are available at metro stations and most drugstores and convenience stores in New York City. They are also available for printing from the Manhattan Transportation Authority's website. If you cannot find a portable metro map, large maps are posted for **reference** in each metro station.

Step 2:

Determine the metro stop nearest to your location and the one nearest to your destination. Not all trains stop at every station, even if both trains are on the same line. For instance, the A, C and E trains stop at the 42nd Street-Times Square Station, but only the C and E trains stop at the 50th Street-8th Avenue Station, even though all three trains are on the same line. On the metro map, an open circle means that all trains on the line stop at the station. A darkened circle means that only local trains stop there. The conductor will state whether you are on a local or express train when you board.

Step 3:

Purchase a Metrocard, which is required for riding the metro, according to the **Metropolitan Transit Authority**. You can purchase a Metrocard from the station **attendant booth** with cash, or buy one with cash or a credit or debit card at an automated Metrocard machine in the lobby. As of 2010, a one-way fare, including transfers to any other metro line, is $2.25. You can put as much or as little money as you want on the Metrocard, which can be used for future metro or bus fares.

Step 4:

Swipe your Metrocard at the turnstile by sliding your card with the black strip to the left. If you are in a wheelchair or have a large suitcase or stroller, alert the metro attendant, who will open a side door to let you in. Otherwise, pass through the turnstile.

Step 5:

Follow the signs for the train line you would like to ride. Most train lines go in two directions, uptown and downtown. If you are traveling north of your current location, you need to travel uptown. If you are traveling south of your current location, you need to travel downtown. Two train lines, the S and the L, travel from east to west. Consult the map to determine whether you need to travel east or west from your destination on these trains.

Step 6:

Wait for your train. Metro trains run every two to five minutes during rush hours and about every 10 minutes during the day, states the NYU Students Guide. After midnight, trains might come less frequently and most express trains run locally.

Step 7:

Step onto the train after all departing passengers have gotten off. If you are traveling late at night, choose a train car that has other passengers and is near the front of the train.

Step 8:

Listen to the announcement for your stop. Metro stations are also clearly marked with the name of the station on the wall where it comes to a stop.

http://traveltips.usatoday.com/ride-nyc-metro-4236.html

Words & Expressions

frugal /ˈfruːgl/ *adj.* （对金钱、食物等）节约的；节俭的

nerve-wracking *adj.* 令人焦虑的

reference /ˈrefrəns/ *n.* 提到；谈及；涉及；参考；查询

metropolitan /ˌmetrəˈpɒlɪtən/ *adj.* 大城市的；大都会的；本土的

attendant booth 服务台

M6-7

After reading, write T for True and F for false.

(　　) 1. There are 26 train lines in New York City.

(　　) 2. Metro maps are only available at metro stations.

(　　) 3. All trains stop at every station.

(　　) 4. On the metro map, a darkened circle means that all trains on the line stop at the station.

(　　) 5. You can purchase a Metrocard from the station attendant booth only with cash.

(　　) 6. Metro trains run every two to five minutes during rush hours and about every 10 minutes during the day.

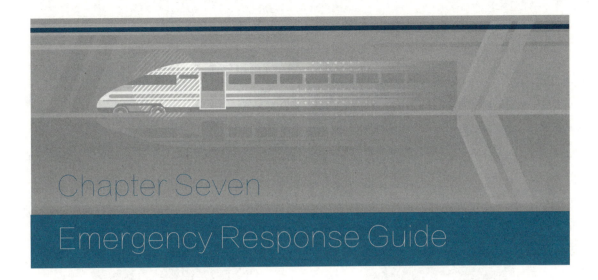

Chapter Seven
Emergency Response Guide

Learning Outcomes

On completion of the module, you will be able to:
1. Know how to deal with emergency events calmly and appropriately
2. Get familiar with the names of emergency facilities
3. Correctly guide the passengers in an event of emergency
4. Guide the passengers to evacuate safely and orderly

Overview of the Module

When riding the train, you may meet some kinds of emergency. One of the top training tasks for the metro crew is to know how to react to the emergency. It's also necessary for passengers to get to know how to deal with the emergency and how to evacuate with the help of the metro staff.

This chapter aims at helping metro staff to get familiar with different reactions in the event of emergency, such as earthquake, fire, explosions, accidents and other situations. In this way, it can help the metro staff appropriately guide passengers to evacuate and decrease casualties in metro stations.

Unit 1
An Earthquake in a Metro Station

What You Will Learn in This Unit

1. Introduction of emergency equipment
2. Response to an earthquake in a metro station

Part I Getting Started

1. Please write down the correct English names for the following pictures.

（1）地震 _____　（2）紧急出口 _____

（3）紧急停车按钮 _____　（4）警报装置 _____

2. Can you list some emergency equipment in a metro station?

Part II　Studying

A. Conversation

Mark is talking with one of the metro staff. He is curious about the response to the emergency in a metro station and the metro worker is explaining it to Mark.

Mark: Hi, I am Mark from Fudan University. I am interested in some emergency instructions in the metro stations. I want to know what we should do if there is an earthquake.

M7-1

SM: Okay, welcome to the Shanghai Metro. When there is an earthquake, there is a possibility that something may fall from the ceiling. It's important to try to stay still and protect your head. If you have a bag with you, it may be a good idea to use it to shield your head while you crouch down in a stable position.

Mark: Okay, what should we do once the quake stops?

SM: Once the quake stops, the station staff will guide you towards the emergency exits. Please remain calm and follow their instructions. Also remember that there can be aftershocks and blackouts following an earthquake, so you shouldn't use the escalators or elevators, as they may pose a threat to your safety.

Mark: Thanks, and what should I do if a quake strikes while we are in the carriage?

SM: Well, in order to avoid falling over, tightly hold on to any bars or straps overhead. When earthquake detectors sense a quake above a certain magnitude, the carriage will stop.

Mark: What should I do after the quake is over?

SM: Depending on the size of the quake, the train may resume service at a slower speed, otherwise it may stop in the tunnel, and you will need to follow the cabin crew's instructions.

Mark: OK. Thanks a lot!

SM: Actually, there is comparatively little danger of metro collapsing with earthquakes. The most dangerous thing is panic. Even if there is a blackout, trains run on to the next station by inertia. Emergency lights will go on as well, so the most important thing is to keep calm and follow the staff's instructions.

Mark: I got it! I appreciate your time in explaining this to me. Thank you so much!

SM: You are welcome!

B. Words & Expressions

earthquake /'ɜːθkweɪk/ *n.* 地震
collision /kə'lɪʒn/ *n.* 冲突
ambulance /'æmbjələns/ *n.* 救护车
safety procedure 安全规程
poisonous gas 毒气
power outage 断电

electric shock 触电
emergency exit 紧急出口
emergency alarm 警报装置
unlikely event 意外事件
safety kit 急救包

M7-2

C. Notes

1. 按下按钮。
Press the button.

2. 按住按钮。
Hold the button.

3. 保持冷静。
Stay calm.

4. 不要恐慌。
Do not panic.

5. 保持耐心。
Be patient.

6. 跟我走。
Follow me.

Part III Your Turn

A. Discussion

1. How should the metro staff react in the case of an earthquake?
2. How should the passengers react in the case of an earthquake in the metro station?

B. Reading Practice

WHAT TO DO IN AN EARTHQUAKE

If possible, "Drop, Cover and Hold On" until the shaking stops.

Stay on board buses and trains or in train stations until instructed to do otherwise by Metro personnel.

The safest place to be during an earthquake is on the underground Metro system—you may not even know an earthquake has occurred.

IF YOU ARE ON A TRAIN OR IN A STATION

The operator will stop the train until the shaking stops and make appropriate announcements to the passengers to keep them informed.

If you are in a train or station of the Metro's underground system, you might not be aware an earthquake is occurring. Sensors will alert Metro personnel that an earthquake is underway, and emergency procedures will go into effect. If the **magnitude** of the earthquake is **sufficient** to cause damage to rail **infrastructure**, automatic shutdown will occur.

Once it is safe to do so, the train will proceed at a reduced speed to the next station with street level trains avoiding all underground areas, elevated stations and all stations under overhead structures.

If the train cannot proceed and it is safe to remain where you are, the operator will assist you in evacuating to a safe location.

Depending upon the magnitude of the earthquake, rail system maintenance engineers may be **dispatched** to **inspect** the system before the train can proceed. Transportation field supervisors will be sent out to assist with any inspections or evacuations required.

Radio dispatch will be monitoring the rail system to handle any emergencies, broadcast instructions to the operators and allow them to proceed along the route when it is safe.

Words & Expressions

magnitude /ˈmæɡnɪtjuːd/ *n.* 巨大；重大；重要性；规模；幅度

sufficient /səˈfɪʃnt/ *adj.* 足够的；充足的

infrastructure /ˈɪnfrəstrʌktʃə(r)/ *n.* (国家或机构的) 基础设施；基础建设

dispatch /dɪˈspætʃ/ *v.* 派遣；调遣；派出

inspect /ɪnˈspekt/ *v.* 检查；查看

M7-3

After reading, write T for True and F for False.

(　　) 1. You should run out of the train station immediately when an earthquake happens in the metro.

(　　) 2. If you are in a train or station of Metro's underground system, you might be strongly aware an earthquake is occurring.

(　　) 3. Once it is safe to do so, the train will proceed at a reduced speed to the next station.

(　　) 4. If the train cannot proceed and it is safe to remain where you are, the operator will assist you in evacuating to a safe location.

(　　) 5. Radio dispatch will be monitoring the rail system to handle any emergencies.

Unit 2
A Fire in a Metro Station

What You Will Learn in This Unit

1. Introduction of emergency fire equipment
2. Responses to fire in metros

3. How to use a fire extinguisher

Part I Getting Started

Please write down the correct English names for the following pictures.

（1）火警按钮 _____ （2）灭火器 _____

（3）医疗救助 _____ （4）消防员 _____

Part II Studying

A. Conversation

Over the telecom

A: Hello? Anyone there? Can you hear me?

C: Yes, Sir. This is the Chengdu Metro. Is there a problem?

A: There's a fire!

C: Sir, calm down. I didn't catch that clearly. Did you say fire?

A: YES! There's a fire! FIRE!

C: Stay calm. I will contact the operator immediately. In the meantime, I have to ask you and other passengers to move to another car where it is safer and away from the fire.

A: What?

C: Please move away from the fire, Sir.

A: Okay.

C: In case the fire spreads, the fire extinguisher is located at the junction of two carts. Do you know how to use a fire extinguisher?

M7-4

A: Not really.

C: It's simple. Follow these instructions strictly. First, pull the safety pin, then aim the nozzle at the base of the fire. Squeeze the handle and sweep the nozzle side to side. Do you get that, Sir?

A: Pull, aim, then shoot?

C: Pull, aim, squeeze, and then sweep. Remember, PASS.

A: I think I can manage it. Pull, aim, squeeze, sweep.

C: Excellent, Sir. The train operator will stop at the next station to let all passengers out. Once the train arrives at the platform, the staff will be there to take care of the passengers. Please stay calm and thank you.

B. Words & Expressions

report /rɪˈpɔːt/ v. 报道
guide /gaɪd/ v. 引导
corrosive /kəˈrəʊsɪv/ adj. 腐蚀性的
firearm /ˈfaɪərɑːm/ n. 枪支
ammunition /ˌæmjuˈnɪʃn/ n. 弹药

fire hazard 火灾
fire alarm button 火警按钮
prohibited item 禁止携带的物品
sharp object 尖锐物品

M7-5

C. Notes

1. 请耐心等待进一步指示/通知。
Wait calmly for further instructions/announcement.

2. 拉下手柄。
Pull down the handle.

3. 快速移动。
Move quickly.

4. 安全第一。
Safety first.

Part III Your Turn

A. Discussion

1. Do you know where fire alarm buttons are located at the platform and on the train?
2. When is it necessary to push the train emergency stop button?
3. What should we do if the platform screen doors do not open automatically?
4. What do you need to tell passengers in case of an emergency evacuation?
5. What do you have to do in case of a fire?
6. What do you have to tell passengers when there's a power outage?
7. What do you have to say and do in order to keep passengers from panicking?

B. Question

Do you know how to use a fire extinguisher? Do you know how to instruct a passenger how to use a fire extinguisher?

怎样使用灭火器？怎样指导乘客使用灭火器？

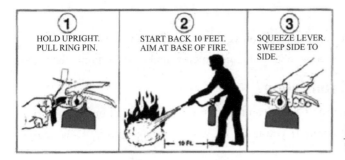

C. Reading Practice

The Emergency Evacuation in MTA New York City Transit

In the event of an emergency that requires evacuating a train, MTA New York City Transit needs you to follow some simple rules to **facilitate** getting you to a safe place. Remember that your best protection is to remain calm, think clearly, and follow the instructions of the train crew.

Always contact a train crew member and listen for announcements.

In the event of an emergency, it may become necessary to evacuate the train you are riding on. Remember to listen to the instructions given by train crews or other emergency responders who will tell you what to do.

There are four ways you may be evacuated from a train to a safe area.

1. Evacuating to Benchwall

The train crew and other emergency personnel will assist you to the area of the tracks **adjacent** to the train known as the Benchwall and lead you to an Emergency Exit or station platform.

2. Transferring to a train ahead or behind

Train crews and other emergency personnel will assist you in transferring from the train you were riding to another train that has pulled up ahead or behind.

3. Transferring to a train alongside

Train crews and other emergency personnel will assist you from the train you were riding to another train that has pulled up alongside. A device will be placed to enable you to move directly into the other train.

4. Evacuating to the **track bed**

Once power is removed, train crews and other emergency personnel will assist you in evacuating to the track bed and leading you safely to an Emergency Exit or station platform.

Words & Expressions

facilitate /fəˈsɪlɪteɪt/ v. 促进；促使；使便利
adjacent /əˈdʒeɪsnt/ adj. 与……毗连的；邻近的
track bed 轨道路基

M7-6

After reading, write T for True and F for False.

(　　) 1. Use the emergency brake cord only when the motion of the metro presents an imminent danger to life and limb.

(　　) 2. Don't try to leave the train without instructions or help from the train crew when there is a fire.

(　　) 3. When there is a fire, attempt to leave the train on your own as fast as you can.

(　　) 4. If there is an emergency, look for a member of the metro crew and report it immediately.

D. What's Wrong with This Translation?

Read the following passage provided in Chinese and then look at the translation. Do you think there's something wrong with the translation? If you think so, what's wrong with it? How can you make it more relevant to the passage?

阅读：

如在地铁车站内发生火灾等紧急情况时，我们要做到五个要诀：

（1）及时报告。利用车站站台墙上的手动火灾报警按钮，或直接报告给地铁车站工作人员，以便车站工作人员及时采取相关措施进行处理。

（2）尽可能找到简易防护。可用毛巾、口罩蒙鼻，最好是湿的。在有浓烟的情况下，采用低姿撤离，贴近地面逃离是避免烟气吸入的最佳方法。视线不清时，手摸墙壁徐徐撤离。

（3）紧急情况下要保持镇定。不能盲目乱跑，要听从工作人员的指挥或广播指引，迎着新鲜空气跑。身上着火，千万不要奔跑，可就地打滚或用厚重的衣物压灭火苗。

（4）遇火灾不可乘坐车站的垂直电梯。

（5）不要贪恋财物，不要因为顾及贵重物品而错过宝贵的逃生时间。

Five things you should remember to do in case of fire and other emergencies:

(1) Tell someone when it's already passed. Press the fire alarm button or use the telecom to notify passengers at the last station.

(2) Look for things around you to use as decorations. Take off your scarves and clothes when it's too hot. Wet them, if you need to. Stand as high as you can to get close to the ceiling. Make sure you can smell the smoke in the air. Touch the wall when you want to stop. Run as fast as you can.

(3) Go wild and run as fast as you can. Always get to the front of the line. Don't listen to what the Metro staff tells you. It's your life, not theirs.

(4) Use the elevators. It's faster.

(5) Take everything with you. They're expensive.

Unit 3
An Explosion in a Metro Station

What You Will Learn in This Unit

1. Inflammable items and explosive items in metro

2. Response in the event of explosion

Part I   Getting Started

Please write down the correct English names for the following pictures.

（1）易燃物品 _____   （2）易爆物品 _____

Part II Studying

A. Conversation

Ben and his friend are waiting at the Wudaokou Train Station. They are now planning to go to National Library Station. Suddenly, they see some passengers running away. So they try to figure out what happened.

M7-7

Ben: Excuse me, what happened? Why are you running away?

Passenger: I heard somebody scream, "bomb, bomb". Then I just ran quickly.

Ben: OK, I think we should keep calm first, and then try to seek help from the train crew. It's dangerous to run in the station. You see, the screen shows the train will arrive in 2 minutes. I will go to find the train crew. Please take care!

Then Ben tries to find one of the train crew to figure out what happened.

Ben: Excuse me, we want to know what happened. Is there really a bomb?

SM: Well, someone told us he found a suspicious bag emitting some sound. We are getting close to check it.

Ben: Okay, I think it's dangerous to run away in the train station. So I think you'd better make an announcement to keep calm.

SM: Thank you for your warning. My colleague is making an announcement soon. We will try to tell passengers to keep calm first, and then evacuate them to a safe place. The train will proceed to the next station.

Ben: You are doing a great job. What can I do for you?

SM: Thanks. However, I hope you can go to the safe place first. After we check the bag, we will make another announcement to the passengers again. Take care!

Ben: Take care.

After a few minutes, the metro staff member checks the suspicious bag. It turns out to be tricks played by a stranger. There is just a clock in the bag.

Announcement: Ladies and gentlemen, we are so sorry to bring such inconvenience to you. We've checked the bag, which is just a normal bag with a clock inside. Someone is playing a trick on us.

Therefore, our train will resume the normal train schedule. Thanks for your cooperation.

B. Words & Expressions

suspicious /sə'spɪʃəs/ *adj.* 可疑的
designate /'dezɪgneɪt/ *v.* 指定
emit /ɪ'mɪt/ *v.* 发出；发射
evacuate /ɪ'vækjueɪt/ *v.* 撤离；疏散
recover /rɪ'kʌvə(r)/ *v.* 恢复
Medical Assistance 医疗救助
inflammable item 易燃物品
be aware of 意识到

figure out 解决；弄明白
keep calm 保持冷静
emit the sound 发出声响
make an announcement 通告
play a trick on 恶作剧
proceed to the next station 继续开到下一站
figure it out 弄明白

M7-8

Part III Your Turn

A. Discussion

Work in groups and discuss the following topics:
1. In case of explosion, what will the metro staff try to do?
2. What will the passengers do in case of explosion?

B. Reading Practice

Emergency Alarm in the U. S.

Press for Emergencies Only

The Emergency Alarm (EA) is a long yellow bar located above the windows of a metro train, along the wheelchair positions and at each end of the metro cars. The Emergency Alarm should be used if a customer needs emergency medical, police or fire services. When the Emergency Alarm is **activated**, the train proceeds to the next station. **Transit Control** is made aware of the alarm and **notifies** 911. Whenever an Emergency Alarm is activated, services will be delayed anywhere from 2 to 20 minutes, depending on the nature or urgency of the incident. Misuse of the Emergency Alarm can result in a significant fine.

Designated Waiting Area (DWA)

Customers who feel unwell on a train should get off the train at the next station and use the intercom at the Designated Waiting Area on the platform. The Station Collector will dispatch help as required.

Designated Waiting Areas are located on all station platforms. The DWA is equipped with intercom access to the station collector, benches, railing, enhanced lighting, CCTV cameras and a **payphone**.

Intercoms are located in Designated Waiting Areas, in elevator cabs, at elevator landings and at entrances not staffed by Station Collectors. They let you talk directly to the Station Collector.

Words & Expressions

activate /ˈæktɪveɪt/ v. 使活动；激活；使活化
transit control 交通管制
notify /ˈnəʊtɪfaɪ/ v.（正式）通报；通知

payphone /ˈpeɪˌfəʊn/ 公用（付费）电话

M7-9

After reading, write T for True and F for False.

(　) 1. The Emergency Alarm should be used if a customer needs emergency medical, police or fire services.

(　) 2. When the Emergency Alarm is activated, the train will stop immediately.

(　) 3. Whenever an Emergency Alarm is activated, services will be delayed anywhere from 2 to 20 minutes.

(　) 4. Misuse of the Emergency Alarm can result in nothing.

(　) 5. Customers who feel unwell on a train should get off the train at the next station.

(　) 6. Designated Waiting Areas are located on most station platforms.

Unit 4
An Accident in a Metro Station

What You Will Learn in This Unit

1. How to respond in the event of accident
2. How to evacuate in the event of an accident

Part I　Getting Started

Please write down the correct English names for the following pictures.

(1) 对讲机 _____　　(2) 地铁控制中心 _____

(3) 紧急门 _____ (4) 紧急疏散 _____

Part II Studying

A. Conversation

Paul is invited to learn something about the reactions to accidents in the Shanghai Metro. The metro staff will introduce what the passengers are supposed to do in the case of an accident.

M7-10

SM: Hi, Paul. So nice to meet you! How are you doing?

Paul: Pretty good. Thanks. How are you?

SM: Good. Welcome to the Shanghai Metro Station. Today I would like to tell you how our metro staff helps passengers to escape from an accident in a metro station.

Paul: Thanks. For our passengers, when an accident happens, the first impression is to run away immediately.

SM: Actually, we hope our passengers will keep calm first, and then follow the instructions of the train operator, or other metro employees or emergency responders.

Paul: OK, what are the basic rules to follow?

SM: OK, first, please contact the train operator by using one of the intercoms at each end of the rail car. And open the emergency doors. Once clear of the train, walk along the walkway toward the nearest station.

Paul: How can we contact the Metro's Operations Control Center?

SM: Okay, to communicate with the Metro's Operations Control Center, you can just open the call box and dial "0", and then cross the tracks. The staircases lead to overhead doors. Push them open to reach the surface.

Paul: Thanks for your explanation. Are metro stations and trains equipped with emergency lights that activate in case of an accident?

SM: Yes. Batteries will provide emergency lights and communication on trains for about two hours.

Paul: Thank you so much! Yeah, I think I know what I am supposed to do in case of an accident. And I can even help others in need.

SM: Thanks for your cooperation.

B. Words & Expressions

employee /emˈplɔiː/ *n.* 雇工
employer /ɪmˈplɔɪə/ *n.* 雇主
reaction /rɪˈækʃn/ *n.* 反应
escape /ɪˈskeɪp/ *v.* 逃离
contact /kənˌtækt/ *v.* 联系
staircase /ˈsteəkeɪs/ *n.* 楼梯
release /rɪˈliːs/ *v.* 释放；放开；放走
life-threatening *adj.* 威胁生命的
train operator 列车操作员

Metro's Operations Control Center 地铁控制中心
emergency door 紧急门
emergency evacuation 紧急疏散
emergency light 紧急灯
be supposed to 应该
be quipped with 使……装备……
in case of 万一，如果

M7-11

Part III Your Turn

A. Discussion

Work in groups and role-play.

Two students work in a group playing out a passenger and a staff member, and trying to figure out what a metro staff member can do to help the passengers to evacuate.

B. Reading Practice

Evacuating a Train in a Tunnel

In almost all situations, evacuation of a train should be performed only under the **supervision** of the train operator, other Metro employees or emergency responders. If the situation is life-threatening and an immediate evacuation is necessary, follow the instructions below:

1. Contact the operator

Before attempting to open the doors, contact the train operator by using one of the intercoms at each end of the rail car. Push the button to speak, release it to listen. Tell the operator your train car number and describe the problem briefly and clearly. Follow the operator's instructions. If you don't get a response immediately, wait and try again. The operator may be communicating with Metro's Operations Control Center or may temporarily be outside the train.

2. Open the emergency doors

Each car has three sets of **automatic doors**. The middle doors can be opened using the emergency door release on the car wall next to the center doors. Look for the raised walkway on the lighted side of the tunnel and use the emergency door release on that side. Lift the panel and pull down on the red handle. Then slide the left door panel open and step down onto the walkway.

3. Stay on the walkway

Once clear of the train, walk along the walkway toward the nearest station (**metallic** signs on the tunnel wall indicate the distance). If a train approaches while you're on the walkway, put your back, arms and legs against the wall until it passes. Watch out for parts of the walkway marked with black and white lines and labeled "No Clearance." In those areas, there is not enough room for a train to pass you safely.

4. Use the call box

Every 800 feet along the **tunnel** walkway there is a call box with a blue light on top. To communicate with Metro's Operations Control Center, open the box and dial "0."

5. Crossing the tracks

At intervals, the walkway switches from one side of the tunnel to the other—or may run between two sets of tracks. To get from one walkway to another, cross the track bed, being careful to avoid all metal objects and water. Also watch for equipment in the track bed, which may pose a tripping **hazard**.

6. Avoid the rails

The third rail—**identifiable** in most places by its white cover plate—is the **conduit** that powers the train. Its 750 volts of direct current is enough to kill instantly if touched. Do not sit or stand on the cover plate. The running rails—the tracks on which the train wheels roll—carry an electric current as well as also must be avoided. Even if a power outage affects the tunnel lights, electricity may continue to course through the rails. If you must walk in the track bed, use extreme care.

7. Emergency exits

If you come to an emergency before reaching a station (they're located every 2,500 feet in the tunnels and are marked with lighted exit signs), exit that way, unless you have been instructed otherwise by Metro or emergency personnel. The staircases lead to overhead doors. Push them open to reach the surface.

Ground-Level or Above-Ground Evacuation

Exiting a Metro train outdoors may seem less **daunting** than evacuating in a tunnel, but passengers should exercise caution and leave the train only if instructed or if it becomes absolutely necessary. As with tunnel evacuations, the first step should be to attempt to conduct the operator from the train's intercom. If an evacuation is necessary, look for the following details to choose which side of the train to exit.

On an elevated track: Find the side with a railing or walking. Open the middle doors using the emergency door release. On ground level: Exit on the side away from the other set of tracks and the third rail. As with tunnels, there are emergency phones located every 800 feet on the ground and on raised walkways. If you are unable to contact Metro staff for instructions, walk to the next station.

Words & Expressions

tunnel /ˈtʌnl/ *n.* 地下通道；地道；隧道
supervision /ˌsuːpəˈvɪʒn/ *n.* 监督；管理
automatic door 自动门
metallic /məˈtælɪk/ *adj.* 金属般的；有金属味（或声音）的
identifiable /aɪˌdentɪˈfaɪəbl/ *adj.* 可识别的；可辨认的

conduit /ˈkɒndjuɪt/ *n.* （液体、气体或电线的）管道；导管
daunting /ˈdɔːntɪŋ/ *adj.* 使人畏惧的；令人胆怯的；让人气馁的

M7-12

After reading, write T for True and F for False.

(   ) 1. Before attempting to open the doors, contact the train operator by using one of the intercoms at each end of the rail car.

(   ) 2. Each car has one set of automatic doors.

(   ) 3. If a train approaches while you're on the walkway, put your back, arms and legs against the wall until it passes.

(   ) 4. Every 800 feet along the tunnel walkway there is a call box with a red light on top.

(   ) 5. To communicate with Metro's Operations Control Center, open the box and dial "9".

Unit 5
Other Situations

What You Will Learn in This Unit

1. Different emergent situations
2. How to respond to different emergency situations

Part I Getting Started

Please write down the correct English names for the following pictures.

(1) _____   (2) _____

(3) _____   (4) _____

Part II Studying

Different emergencies require different responses. Know how to react and what to expect.

1. Q: If there's an evacuation emergency, will the Metro run on a rush-hour schedule regardless of the date?

A: If possible, Metro would ramp up service during an emergency. But you should not assume Metro could simultaneously take care of everyone who drove into the city as well as those who commuted via Metro. In fact, it can't. Be prepared to shelter in place or get home in another way.

2. Q: If we have to evacuate a station, will all the exit gates in the station be open, or will the passengers have to find their farecards?

A: Most likely they will be open. If an alarm inside a station is triggered by smoke or heat, the fare gates will open automatically. The gates will also open on their own during a power outage. The station manager can open all the gates from the kiosk; he can switch the escalators so most or all run upward as well.

3. Q: Are Metro stations and trains equipped with emergency lights that activate in case of a power failure?

A: Yes. Batteries will provide emergency lights and communication on trains for about two hours. Emergency lighting and communication, as well as other functions, can continue for at least three hours in stations and parking garages. Tunnels have at least three hours of emergency lighting, though at a reduced level. Few elevators and escalators would move, but Metro's Operations Control Center would know the location of the train, and if the operator couldn't be reached, personnel would be dispatched.

4. Q: If we're waiting in an underground station and there's an event in the upper station — an explosion, a fire, a chemical attack — should we seek cover in the tunnel? Take a train to the next station?

A: Generally, you should not seek refuge in the tunnel. And chances are good that trains would stop running, at least for a little while. Check first for guidance from the station manager, Metro staff or responders. Underground stations with only one exit also have emergency exits at either or both ends of the platform, which can be used if the main exit is unreachable. They are marked with illuminated exit signs.

5. Q: Are any Metro stations equipped with defibrillators in case someone has a heart attack? Where are they located?

A: Defibrillators are installed at all Virginia stations, and in the District at Metro Center, Gallery Place, Chinatown, L'Enfant Plaza, Judiciary Square, McPherson Square, Foggy Bottom, Smithsonian, Farragut North and Farragut West. The eventual goal is to place them in all stations. The defibrillators are kept either in the manager's kiosk or in a cabinet nearby. Riders should seek the manager if they think a defibrillator is needed.

6. Q: In an emergency on a train, what will happen to those in strollers and wheelchairs if we have to get out and walk?

A: Wheelchairs and strollers are probably too big for the tunnel's walkway, so they may need to be left behind. If that's the case, Metro will try to recover them when the emergency is over. For those who can't walk, means of evacuation could include being carried or placed on one of the evacuation carts that are stored throughout the tunnels. The carts roll on the two running rails and can transport four people at a time or up to 1,000 pounds. Fire departments also have equipment such as plastic sleds that can be used to carry passengers.

7. Q: What should I do if I see a suspicious package left on a train while it's at a station? Should I push it off onto the platform?

A: No. If you see a package that seems suspicious, you should use one of the intercoms at either end of the Metro car to report it to the train operator. Moving the bag could endanger more people — and send Metro police out looking for you as a suspect.

8. Q: Can the Metro be closed off completely and used as a shelter in case of a terrorist attack aboveground?

A: No. You should not attempt to use the system as a refuge in an aboveground attack. Metro stations are not approved shelters for chemical, biological or radiological attacks. Sheltering in place — whether at home or work.

Words & Expressions

assume /əˈsjuːm/ v. 假设
simultaneously /ˌsɪmlˈteɪniəsli/ adv. 同时地
shelter /ˈʃeltə(r)/ n. 遮蔽；避难所
　　　　v. 躲避；避难
trigger /ˈtrɪɡə(r)/ v. 引发；触发；发射或使爆炸
automatically /ˌɔːtəˈmætɪkli/ adv. 自动地
switch /swɪtʃ/ v. 转换
defibrillator /diːˈfaɪbrɪˌleɪtə(r)/ n. （电击）除颤器

illuminate /ɪˈluːmɪneɪt/ v. 照明
battery /ˈbætəri/ n. 电池
rush-hour schedule 高峰时刻表
parking garage 停车库
chemical/biological/radiological attack 化学/生物/放射物质攻击

M7-13

Part III　Your Turn

Group Discussion

1. If we have to evacuate a station, will the exit gates in the station all be open?
2. If we're waiting in an underground station and there's an event in the upper station—an explosion, a fire, a chemical attack—should we seek cover in the tunnel?
3. In an emergency on a train, what will happen to those in strollers and wheelchairs if we have to get out and walk?
4. What should I do if I see a suspicious package left on a train while it's at a station?
5. Can the Metro be closed off completely and used as a shelter in case of a terrorist attack aboveground?
6. Are Metro stations and trains equipped with emergency lights that activate in case of a power failure?

Chapter Eight
Foreign Country Metro Outlook

On completion of the module, you will be able to:
1. Know the metro service in developed countries
2. Know the metro service in developing countries

Overview of the Module

The metro systems in different countries are different. They usually refer to electrified rapid transit train systems. Now, about 148 cities in 55 countries around the world host the approximately 160 metro systems. The earliest metro system is the London Underground, which was opened as an underground railway in 1863. The metro system with the longest route length in the world is the Shanghai Metro. The busiest one is the Beijing Metro, and the one with the most stations is the New York City Metro.

This chapter focuses on introduction of different metro systems in main cities among developed countries and developing countries. It mainly introduces the fares, safety services and train lines. It helps readers better understand the metro system in different countries.

Unit 1
The Metro System in Developed Countries

What You Will Learn in This Unit
1. The introduction of the metro system in U.S.A.
2. The introduction of the metro system in the U K.
3. The introduction of the metro system in Dubai
4. The introduction of the metro system in Japan

Part I Getting Started

Can you write down the countries' names of the following metro cards?

(1) _____

(2) _____

(3) _____

(4) _____

Part II Studying

Reading Passage 1

NYC Metro System

U.S. metro areas overall were home to about 272.7 million people in 2014, an increase of roughly 2.4 million from 2013. And of the nation's 381 metro areas, 298 gained population last year. New York remains the most populous U. S. metro area, with the region home to about 20.1 million people last year. The New York City Metro is one of the world's oldest public transit systems, one of the world's most used metro systems, and the metro system with the most stations and the most **trackage**. The New York City metro system is also one of the most efficient people transports in the entire world. Over 4.3 million people ride the metro system every day; over 1 billion people go through the turnstiles per year! It offers rail service 24 hours per day and every day of the year. The New York City Metro is the largest rapid transit system in the world by number of stations, with 468 stations in operation. Stations are located throughout the **boroughs** of Manhattan, Brooklyn, Queens, and the Bronx. The system is also one of the world's longest. Overall, the system contains 232 miles (373 km) of routes, translating into 656 miles (1,056 km) of revenue track; and a total of 842 miles (1,355 km) including non-**revenue** trackage.

FARES

The primary method of **fare** payment is the Metrocard. All metro stations and buses are now Metrocards **capable**. Tokens are also available, and cost $2.00 each. Metrocards can be bought on a pay-per-ride basis ($2.00 per ride) or an **unlimited ride** basis. With pay-per-ride, you get 11 rides for the price of ten and you can add more money to your card if need be. With unlimited ride MetroCards, you can get a 30-day card, a 7-day card, or a 1-day Fun Pass. Children under 44cm tall ride for free; **senior citizens** and disabled people ride for a **reduced fare**.

RIDING THE METRO WITH A NEW YORK METRO CARD

New York metro system can be a bit intimidating at first, and the locals do rush around to make you feel the pressure from someone right behind you in line getting even more impatient. To enter, you have to swipe your MetroCard through a **reader** and then wait for the display to say, "go". Unfortunately, this isn't as easy as it sounds at times. It can be kind of **tricky** at first, but if you can't seem to get it working, you are not alone. Just watch other people and do what they do.

SAFETY

For many **decades**, the New York City metro system had a reputation for being dirty and dangerous. The famous **graffiti** are long gone, but the stations and **carriages** sometimes still do suffer from people unable to find **abundant** station trashcans. The biggest problem is the safety issue. However, there is some good news coming as well. The amount of crime reported throughout the system is way down from its **peak**, but that's not to say you shouldn't be cautious.

Words and Expressions

trackage /ˈtrækɪdʒ/ *n.* 轨道；轨长
borough /ˈbʌrə/ *n.* 区；自治的市镇
fare /feə(r)/ *n.* 公共交通费
capable /ˈkeɪpəbl/ *adj.* 有能力的；有才干的

M8-1

revenue /'revənju:/ n. 财政收入；收益
unlimited ride 不限次数乘坐
senior citizen 老年人
reduced fare 优惠价
reader /'ri:də(r)/ n. 读卡器
tricky /'trɪki/ adj. 狡猾的；棘手的

decade /'dekeɪd; dɪ'keɪd/ n. 十年
carriage /'kærɪdʒ/ n. 客车厢
peak /pi:k/ n. 山峰；顶点
graffiti /grə'fi:ti/n. 墙上乱写乱画的东西（**graffito** 的复数形式）
abundant /ə'bʌndənt/ adj. 丰富的

Discussion

1. Can you generally describe the metro system in NYC?
2. What kinds of unlimited ride MetroCards can you find in NYC?
3. How do you use the MetroCard in NYC?

Reading Passage 2

London Underground System

The London Underground (also known as the Tube or simply the Underground) is a public rapid transit system serving a large part of Greater London and parts of the home counties of Buckinghamshire, Hertfordshire and Essex. The network is considered the oldest rapid transit system, **incorporating** the world's first underground railway, the Metropolitan Railway, which opened in 1863 and is now part of the Circle, Hammersmith & City and Metropolitan lines; and the first line to operate underground **electric traction trains**, the City & South London Railway in 1890, now part of the Northern line. The network has expanded to 11 lines, and in 2013/14 carried 1.265 billion passengers, making the Underground the world's 11th busiest metro system. The system serves 270 stations and has 402 kilometres (250 mi) of track. The following shows The London Underground, which opened in 1863. More than 30,000 passengers tried out the Tube on the opening day and it was **hailed** by the *Times* as "the great engineering **triumph** of the day". Pictured by William Gladstone on An Inspection of the First Underground Line.

London Tube

The London Underground rail network, or "the Tube" is a great way to travel to and from Central London and will be an **integral** part of most people's stay in the UK capital. Greater London is served by 12 Tube lines, along with the Docklands Light Railway (DLR) and an **interconnected** local train network. Underground trains generally run between 5 a. m. and midnight, Monday to Saturday, with **reduced operating hours** on Sunday. From Saturday 12 September 2015, there will be 24-hour Tube service on Friday and Saturday night on the Jubilee, Victoria and most of the Piccadilly, Central and Northern Tube lines.

Fares

Buy a Visitor Oyster card, Oyster card, Travel card or use a **contactless payment** card to get the best value as cash is the most expensive way to pay. An adult cash fare for a single journey in Zone 1 is £4.80. The same fare with Visitor Oyster card, Oyster card or contactless payment card is £2.30. There are various discounts available for children, students and elderly travellers.

Tips for Tube Travellers

Here are some other useful tips that will make your journey more enjoyable and efficient:

• Avoid travelling during rush hours (weekdays, 7:00-9:00 a. m. and 5:30-7:00 p. m.) if at all possible.

• Check the front of the train for the correct destination.

• Stand on the right when using escalators.

• Wait for passengers to leave the train before boarding.

• Stand behind the yellow line whilst waiting for the train on the platform.

• Offer your seat to anyone who is unwell, elderly, pregnant or travelling with small children.

• Hold onto the rails if you are standing during your journey.

• Mind the gap!

Words & Expressions

incorporate /ɪnˈkɔːpəreɪt/ v. 包含；吸收
electric traction train 电力牵引列车
hail /heɪl/ v. 招呼
triumph /ˈtraɪʌmf/ n. 胜利，凯旋
integral /ˈɪntɪgrəl; ɪnˈtegrəl/ adj. 完整的

interconnect /ˌɪntəkəˈnekt/ v. 互相联系
reduced operation hours 减少运行时间
contactless payment 非接触支付

Discussion

1. Please describe the history of London Underground System.
2. Can you please tell us the difference between underground trains' operating hours on weekdays and that on weekends?
3. If you take the tube in London, what tips should you pay attention to?

Reading Passage 3
Dubai Metro System

Dubai inaugurated its metro network in September 2009, becoming the first urban metro network to run in the Gulf's Arab states. The system has eased the daily **commute** for thousands of the workers in the emirate. With an economy increasingly based upon financial services, air transport, property development and tourism, Dubai has a rapidly growing population and severe **traffic congestion** problems. The population is forecast to increase by 6.4% annually, rising to three million by 2017. Dubai Municipality identified the need for a rail system to relieve growing motor traffic levels and support continuing urban development based on studies that began in 1997. The Red Line was the first line to be completed, in April 2010. The Green line was opened in September 2011. Two more lines are planned. The intention is for 320 km of metro lines to be in place in Dubai by 2020. Dubai Metro is the longest **automated driverless system** in the world. In February 2012 the Dubai Metro entered **the Guinness World Records** book as the longest driverless metro network in the world, spanning 74.69 km. In full operation, Dubai Metro is projected to carry **approximately** 1.2 million passengers on an **average** day, and 355 million passengers a year.

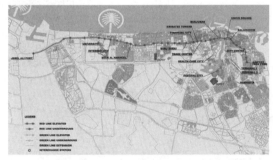

Dubai Metro is one of the most advanced urban rail systems in the world and will be a **catalyst** for tourism, financial and economic growth.

All stations will have **platform doors** to increase safety and allow a more comfortable, climate-controlled environment for passengers.

Fares

Dubai is divided into 5 zones. Each zone has metro, bus and waterbus stations. Journeys can be made using different modes of transport. Tickets prices are cheap compared to similar systems in other major cities. Children aged up to 5 years travel free. Passengers pay with Nol cards. Different types of cards are available to meet individual passengers' needs. Cards must be purchased before travel. The fare is charged at the end of the journey, and is dependent on the number of zones passed through. The fare is deducted when the card is tapped on one of the card readers located at the exits of metro stations, buses or waterbuses. Passes are available and can be charged to cards. 1- , 7- , 30- , 90- , and 365-

The trains have a three-class **layout** and sections of open floor space.

day passes are available. For example: a 1-day pass for a Red ticket costs 20 AED (40 AED for Gold Class). A 7-day Zone 3 pass costs 110 AED (220 AED for Gold Class) while a 30-day Zone 3 pass costs 350 AED (700 AED for Gold Class).

Nol Blue Card　　　　Nol Red Card　　　　Nol Gold Card　　　　Nol Silver Card

Words & Expressions

commute /kəˈmjuːt/ v.（搭乘车、船等）通勤；代偿
traffic congestion 交通拥堵
automated driverless system 全自动无人驾驶系统
the Guinness World Records 吉尼斯世界纪录
approximately /əˈprɒksɪmətli/ adv. 大约；近似地；近于

average /ˈævərɪdʒ/ adj. 平均（数）的；普通的
catalyst /ˈkætəlɪst/ n. [物化] 催化剂；刺激因素
platform door 站台门
layout /ˈleɪaʊt/ n. 布局；设计；安排；陈列

M8-3

Discussion

1. What feature of Dubai Metro helped it enter the Guinness World Records in 2012?
2. How many zones is Dubai divided?
3. What is the age limit for a free ticket?
4. What is the price for different Nol Cards, such as one-day pass, 7-day pass and 30-day pass?

Reading Passage 4

The Tokyo Metro System

　　Tokyo **is blessed with** one of the world's most **efficient** public transportation systems. The Tokyo Metro is a part of the extensive rapid transit system that **consists of** Tokyo Metro and Toei Metro in the Greater Tokyo Area of Japan. While the metro system itself is largely within the city center, the lines extend far out via extensively thorough services onto **suburban** railway lines. As of 2013, the combined metro network of the Tokyo and Toei metros **comprises** 290 stations and 13 lines. The Tokyo Metro and Toei networks together carry a combined average of over eight million passengers daily. The Tokyo Metro opened in 1927. Now Tokyo's metro system carries 8.7 million passengers a day. There are 13 metro lines including 9 Tokyo Metro lines and 4 Toei Metro lines. For ease of use, each station is **coded** with a letter and number. You will find these on platform signs and route maps. It has also introduced women-only carriages during the morning rush hours to provide "a sense of security". Its Metro Manners guidebook advises passengers to set their mobiles to silent mode and **refrain** from talking during the ride.

Fares

Tickets sold at ticket vending machines are found at every Tokyo Metro station. Tickets are available in denominations of 170 yen, 200 yen, 240 yen, 280 yen and 310 yen. Select the fare based on the distance you will travel.

Adult   **Child**

Ticket prices for the metro in Tokyo start at 170 yen with a **paper ticket**, but if you are spending any time in Tokyo it would be wise to **invest** in a Pasmo or Suica **rechargeable** IC card to ease connections between the two systems, save on the wait for buying tickets, and save on fares: the fare using an IC card is up to 5 yen cheaper per ride. A Suica card requires a 500 yen deposit when first issued, but the 500 yen is **refundable** when you have finished with it. The Suica card is usable on JR East lines in Tokyo metropolitan area, all Tokyo metro lines, buses and the Tokyo Monorail that runs between Haneda Airport and Tokyo. Outside Tokyo, the Suica can be used on some transport networks in Hokkaido, Sendai, Niigata, Tokai, west Japan and Kyushu. The Suica can be used in many station kiosks and regular convenience stores to make purchases of goods. Tokyo's metro network connects with other metropolitan rail systems particularly the JR Yamanote Line and, for shinkansen lines, at Tokyo Station and Ueno Station. Again, having a Pasmo or Suica card will make even the transit between metro and above-ground lines effortless and seamless.

Here are some useful hints for using the Tokyo metro system.

1. First buy a pre-paid card, such as a Suica or Pasmo. They require a refundable 500 yen **initial charge**, but make metro use infinitely easier than having to buy a paper ticket at a station whenever you ride a train. You only need to tap your card for a second on the sensor at the ticket wicket as you pass through.

2. **Identify** in advance the number of the exit you need to take at the destination station.

3. Having identified that exit, board the car closest to that destination exit. You will save time (and be less likely to get lost) if you can board the car that will stop closest to the destination station exit you will leave from. There are charts for that purpose on the station wall, telling you the appropriate cars for each exit at each station, or you can ask a station attendant.

4. Mind your manners. Don't eat or drink on the train, don't put luggage on the seat beside you, don't use a cell phone, and if you're talking to people, try and keep it **subdued**.

Words & Expressions

M8-4

be blessed with 在……方面有福；赋有……的
efficient /ɪˈfɪʃnt/ *adj.* 有效率的
consist of 由……组成；由……构成；包括
suburban /səˈbɜːbən/ *adj.* 郊区的，城郊的
comprise /kəmˈpraɪz/ *v.* 包含；由……组成
code /kəʊd/ *n.* 代码；密码
　　　　v. 编码
refrain /rɪˈfreɪn/ *v.* 节制；克制；避免
paper ticket 纸质票

invest /ɪnˈvest/ *v.* 投资；投入
rechargeable /ˌriːˈtʃɑːdʒəbl/ *adj.* 可再充电的；收费的
refundable /rɪˈfʌndəbl/ *adj.* 可退还的；可偿还的
initial charge 起初费用
identify /aɪˈdentɪfaɪ/ *v.* 确定；鉴定；识别，辨认出
subdue /səbˈdjuː/ *v.* 征服；抑制；减轻

Discussion

1. How many passengers does the Tokyo's metro system carry daily?
2. How many metro lines are there in Tokyo's metro system?
3. Can you please tell us some peculiar features of Tokyo's metro system?
4. How much deposit does a Suica card require when first issued?

Unit 2
The Metro System in Developing Countries

What You Will Learn in This Unit

1. The introduction of the metro system in Brazil
2. The introduction of the metro system in Singapore
3. The introduction of the metro system in India

Part I Getting Started

Match the English words with their Chinese meanings.

1. crowded peak hour   A. 不能退票
2. there are no seats available   B. 把卡对准感应器
3. tickets are not refunded   C. 没有座位了
4. touch your card on the sensor   D. 路线图
5. platform sign   E. 高峰拥挤时段
6. route map   F. 站台标示

Part II Studying

Reading Brazil Tram/Metro

Metro systems exist in eight Brazilian cities, including São Paulo, Rio de Janeiro and Belo Horizonte. In others, such as Curitiba, a Bus Rapid Transit system is in operation, which has been praised for being an efficient and eco-friendly means of **intercity transportation**. Coming to Brazil and transiting is quite a headache due to the road-based system in which the country was established. Brazilian governments were never interested in building or expanding railways for metros and trains. Instead, roads took **precedence** in the country, and it became hard to go from city to city—and even from one point of a city to another in the same city—without having a car or depending on buses. Not all the state's capitals have metros. Only 11 out of 27 cities—Belo Horizonte, Brasília, Fortaleza, João Pessoa, Maceió, Natal, Porto Alegre, Recife, Rio de Janeiro, Salvador and São Paulo, which represent less than 1% of the 5565 municipalities in the country—have a system in place. The common factor between these systems is the usage **saturation** i.e., unbelievably crowded. Foreigners who come to Brazil are normally shocked by the **sheer** amount of people using the metro during rush hours. The volume of people is even worse when something is broken or there's been an accident, which is also quite a common situation in Brazil. Notice that by "crowded" we mean "absolutely no space" inside the train car.

São Paulo

In São Paulo, for instance, the train cars get completely full—there are no seats available and people actually **squeeze** themselves against other passengers so they don't have to wait for the next crowded metro. During **peak hours**, it may take more than 1 hour to travel a route that would normally take 20 minutes during non-peak hours. Besides, there is the fact that a lot of Brazilians consider the metro as a mother's heart, where there is always room for one more (even when there is not). So if being really close to another human is not something that you appreciate and you prefer to have your own space, then stay away from São Paulo's metro between 6-8 a. m. and 5-7 p. m. on the workdays.

Rio de Janeiro

Rio de Janeiro's metro also has crowded peak hours, and worse than that, there have been registered cases of rape inside the train cars. The measure taken by the government to avoid this

occurrence was to provide **exclusive** train cars for women during rush hours. Since 2006, during workdays, from 6 to 9 a. m. and 5 to 8 p. m., there is an exclusive car for women. There is no punishment for men who are caught in women's train cars, only for the metro company that doesn't provide the special train car. The system was also **implemented** in Brasília's metro, in July, 2013, and by the same time, São Paulo's government was considering doing the same in the city's metro too. However, as it happened back in Rio in 2006, there's a **criticism** that argues that this is a sexist and stopgap measure. The method projects women as fragile people who can't defend themselves and men as sexually uncontrolled people, and it doesn't actually try to solve the issue, which is men raping women. People who are against the measure say that it legitimates the violence that happens inside the train cars, and that instead governments should provide educational programs to target the root of the problem.

Words & Expressions

intercity transportation 城际交通
precedence /ˈpresɪdəns/ n. 优先；居先
saturation /ˌsætʃəˈreɪʃn/ n. 饱和；浸透
sheer /ʃɪə(r)/ adj. 绝对的；透明的
squeeze /skwiːz/ v. 挤；压榨
peak hours /non-peak hours 高峰时间/非高峰时间

occurrence /əˈkʌrəns/ n. 发生；出现
exclusive /ɪkˈskluːsɪv/ adj. 独有的；排外的
implement /ˈɪmplɪmənt/ v. 实施
criticism /ˈkrɪtɪsɪzəm/ n. 批评

M8-5

Discussion

1. What's the biggest problem of Brazil's metro system?
2. If you take the train in São Paulo, then what time should you stay away from São Paulo's metro on the workdays?
3. What measure did the Rio de Janeiro government take to prevent the cases of rape in the train?

Singapore Metro System

The MRT is a **rapid transit system** and forms the **backbone** of the public transport system of Singapore. The system began operations on 7th November 1987 and presently has 6 lines that serve 113 stations. The network has a total system length of 152.9 km (95 miles). It is operated by SBT Transit (ComfortDelgro Corporation) SMRT Trains (SMRT Corporation). More than 2.7 million people use the MRT daily. The metro service starts operations around 5:30 a.m. and runs until around midnight daily. The frequency of the trains during peak hours from 7-9 a.m. is 2-3 minutes and about 5-7 minutes during off peak hours. During public holidays like Chinese New Year, and festivals like Deepavali and Hari Raya Puasa, the metro services are extended.

Fares

The fares on metro are distance based and riders pay only for the distance they wish to travel. Standard tickets can be purchased for both single and return journeys. The ticket can be used within 30 days from the date of purchase and can be used up to six times. A deposit of 10 cents is included in the purchase price of the ticket, which is refunded on the fare of the third trip. A further discount of 10 cents is also given during the sixth trip. A distance of 10.2 km is charged at $ 1.38 for adult, $ 0.60 for student and $ 0.94 for senior citizen. A distance of 19.2 km is charged at $ 1.74 for adult, $ 0.60 for student and $ 0.94 for senior citizen. And adult fare for a distance of 24 km is priced at $ 1.88, the fare for students for this distance is $ 0.60 and for senior citizens, fare for the same distance is $ 0.94. For a distance of 26 km, adult fare is $ 2.12, student fare is $ 0.60 and senior citizen fare is $ 0.94. An adult fare for a distance of 29 km is priced at $ 1.9, the fare for students for this distance is $ 0.60 and for senior citizens, fare for the same distance is $ 0.94. Adult stored value smart cards can also be used for fare payment.

There are two types of these cards, *EZ-link* and *Nets Flashpay*. These can be purchased from a ticket office or passenger service centers. Children with a height of 0.9 m and below travel free when accompanied by a fare paying adult. Children above the height of 0.9 m and below 7 years of age can obtain *child concession cards,* which provide **discounted rates**. Students under the age of 21, are given student smartcards, which provide student concessionary rates. Senior citizens above the age of 60 can avail *senior citizen cards* that provide 25% concession on adult fares.

Words & Expressions

rapid transit system 快速运输系统
backbone /'bækbəʊn/ *n.* 脊骨；脊柱
discounted rate 打折比例；贴现率

M8-6

Discussion

1. When did the Singapore metro system begin operations?
2. What are the operation hours of Singapore's metro?
3. Can you please describe the metro fares in Singapore?

India Metro

Indian cities are among the world's fastest developing cities in terms of every aspect, population, economy and **infrastructure**. The transport system of India got a new mode called Metro, after its independence, Kolkata was the first city to get a rapid transit system in India. Indian Metro system also has one of the longest metro tunnels in the world; Delhi Metro yellow line has around 3—30 km long underground tunnel. Currently, metro rail projects are running in different parts of the country and Metro and Monorail Transit are proposed for the cities like Lucknow, Kanpur, Patna, Ahmedabad, Pune, Surat, Indore, Nagpur and Bhopal.

Calcutta Metro is the first mass rapid transit system in the country and India's oldest Metro Railway. Line 1 North-South Metro of 25 kilometers is in operation with 23 stations of which 15 are underground stations. Kolkata Metro is also the first in the country to build an operational

underground railway. There were 5 more railway lines **under construction** at the different corners of Calcutta, West Bengal. Chennai was the second city in India to run a rapid transit system in 1995; Chennai Mass Rapid Transit System is an elevated railway line run within the city from Chennai Beach to Velachery.

The Chennai Metro Rail and **monorail network** system will help the city for **reliable** and safe transportation. Chennai Metro Rail project consists of both **elevated** and underground section and was completed in 2013. The National Capital Region of India got another best mode of transportation called rapid transit system; Delhi Metro has 6 lines of 189.63 kilometers with 142 railway stations of which 35 are underground. Delhi Metro consists of a combination of at-grade, underground and elevated lines. Bengaluru Metro also known as Namma Metro has recently started rapid transit rail system in the Bengaluru city of Karnataka. The second phase Namma Metro will also open soon at the end of 2012 and the rest of the phases will be completed as per plan.

Mumbai, the financial and commercial capital of India is all set to provide another mode of transport to people. Mumbai is the largest city in India and needs a mass public transport system. Mumbai Metro and Mumbai Monorail will help the life line of Mumbai called Mumbai Suburban Railway. Mumbai is already running Monorail system, the first monorail in India. Mumbai metro is opened and over 10 lakh commuters traveled on the city's first Metro train.It covers the 11.4 km long journey from the Versova-Andheri-Ghatkopar corridor. Hyderabad Metro is under construction with 3 lines and covering a distance of around 71 km for the city. The **targeted** date for Phase 1 to

be operational from Miyapur to Ameerpet is by December 2014. The Hyderabad Metro is the first public-private **partnership** metro project in India. Hyderabad is already running a Multi-Modal Transport System for particular routes.

The pink city of Rajasthan got its first metro line of 9.2 km from Mansarovar to Chandpole Bazaar in November 2010. Rajasthan is one of the most tourist-visited places in India, especially international tourists and Jaipur is the best place to enjoy royal Rajasthan. The Komet or Kochi Metro is under construction, building a rapid transit system in Kochi city of Kerala. Kochi is one of the fastest developing cities in Kerala state. It has an international airport, harbor and now the Metro.

Words & Expressions

infrastructure /ˈɪnfrəstrʌktʃə(r)/ *n.* 基础设施
under construction 在建造中；正在施工之中
monorail network 单轨网络
reliable /rɪˈlaɪəbl/ *adj.* 可靠的；可信赖的
elevated /ˈelɪveɪtɪd/ *adj.* 提高的；高尚的

targeted /ˈtɑːgɪtɪd/ *adj.* 定向的；被定为攻击目标的
partnership /ˈpɑːtnəʃɪp/ *n.* 合伙；合作关系

M8-7

Discussion

1. What's the new mode called for transport system of India?
2. What's the specific feature of Indian Metro system?
3. What's the first mass rapid transit system in the country?

Chapter Nine
Metro Service Management

On completion of the module, you are supposed to:

1. Know the feature of railway transport
2. Know the modes of railway transport management
3. Know the content of railway transport management

Overview of the Module

Metro service management is as crucial as metro construction. Although metro service greatly reduces city traffic problems and makes the city dynamic with daily large population commuting, it also attracts more investment from outside. The development of Beijing, Shanghai and Guangzhou benefits from their convenient metro network.

However, the features of metro also worry the local authorities, for its huge investment, a long construction period and low profit rate. Without constant government support, metro development can hardly be made. A major contradiction is that government must reduce the investment in metro after its construction because of heavy financial burden.

In this case, the metro must face the changes adapting to the market-oriented operation. Only in this way can it draw the private investor's attention and make the metro service develop constantly.

Unit 1
The Operation Features of Railway Transport

What You Will Learn in This Unit

1. Fast development of operation network
2. Complex rail transport network
3. Diversity of service needs

Part I Studying

A. Conversations

Mary and Xiao Hui are students from Jiaotong University. They were talking about the operation features of railway transport.

Mary: Xiao Hui, I'm really confused about what the teacher said today, especially the operation features of railway transport.

M9-1

Xiao Hui: I can understand some of them. Let's discuss some parts and if we can't solve it, we can ask the teacher for help.

Mary: OK. The first part is about the fast development of the metro service. The teacher gave us some data about the number of passengers in different years. For instance, there were 100,000 passengers in flow volume 10 years ago. However, it rose to around 10 million today. It's incredible. How did this happen?

Xiao Hui was giggling; she knew the reason.

Xiao Hui: Shanghai had a population of around 18 million ten years ago, but there were only 5 lines. It's really hard to meet the passengers' needs. In 2015, there were 14 lines and 2 more were being built. You know it's a real problem to offer commuting service for such a huge population.

Mary: I understand it now. And another question is how to provide good service for the passengers. It's impossible to arrange some trains, sell so many tickets and keep everything in order. The teacher gave us a map of railway transport information system. It's too complicated.

Xiao Hui: The first part we should know is the title of different departments. You can imagine you are a passenger and follow the order like this.

Xiao Hui took out a pencil and drew a picture.

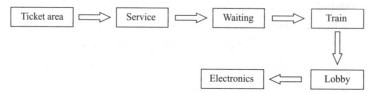

Mary: It's clear. However it's also a problem to arrange so many people in the area.

Xiao Hui: You should know we have PIS, the Passenger Information System, which can provide abundant information for the passengers including metro maps, transfer information, local geographic information, bus stops and even the shopping center. It's installed in every station with a big screen. Anyone can notice that. Besides, the ticket vending machines and automatic turnstiles can supply the effective methods for passengers to take the metro.

Mary: Wow, you are so helpful. I'm quite clear now. Thank you.

Xiao Hui: You are welcome.

B. Words & Expressions

operation /ˌɒpəˈreɪʃn/ *n.* 操作；经营；运转
feature /ˈfiːtʃə(r)/ *n.* 特征；特色
solve /sɒlv/ *v.* 解决；解答
development /dɪˈveləpmənt/ *n.* 发展

M9-2

data /ˈdeɪtə/ n. 数据；资料
incredible /ɪnˈkredəbl/ adj. 难以置信的
provide /prəˈvaɪd/ v. 提供；规定；供应
arrange /əˈreɪndʒ/ v. 整理；安排；布置
title /ˈtaɪtl/ n. 头衔；标题；名称
department /dɪˈpɑːtmənt/ n. 部门；机关；系
imagine /ɪˈmædʒɪn/ v. 想象；猜想；料想
geographic /ˌdʒɪəˈɡræfɪk/ adj. 地理学的；地理的

install /ɪnˈstɔːl/ v. 安装；安置
supply /səˈplaɪ/ v. 补给；提供；供给
effective /ɪˈfektɪv/ adj. 有效的；实际的
method /ˈmeθəd/ n. 方法；秩序；条理
passenger flow volume 旅客流量
keep everything in order 将一切安排得井井有条
railway transport information system 地铁运输信息系统

C. Notes

1. operation features of metro（地铁运营特点）①地铁运营规模：地铁的运营规模在很大程度上影响了地铁运营的调度调整模式，地铁所设计的运营运输能力应与预测的远期单向高峰时段的最大断面客流量需求相匹配。②运营模式：根据地铁的运营特点，地铁线路应保持安全封闭，同时列车运行应以安全防护监控为基础。每一列地铁都应配备一位司机，而客运量不稳定的地铁线路应分区段进行组织，列车的运行线路应按照地铁设计年度客流量断面分布状况确定，地铁线路若为曲线，运营中心可控制和管理一条或者多条地铁线路的实际运行。车站应设有监控室，对列车的运行以及设备状况进行监控，通过采取计程票价制，能同时自动控制客流数据以及票务收入。③地铁运营管理方式：地铁运营的管理应与管理要求和任务相符合，并通过机构合理安排管理，在对地铁运营机构以及地铁人员数量进行安排时，应以地铁运行的科技进步和地铁运行效率提高为实际标准，实现人员和机构的精简。运营管理机构还应针对地铁运营状况制定相应的管理规程和应遵循的规章制度。

2. the operation system in advanced countries（发达国家的运行系统）地铁工程设计一般以100年为标准，根据城市人口、经济、政治等特点，从选线设计、工程建设和运营组织策略方面制定全面、系统的整体方案。综合协调多交通方式衔接，考虑城市公交路线、城际铁路和通勤铁路的衔接问题。另外考虑从郊区到市中心客流特点，立足整个城市公共交通，根据城市地区发展和客流情况，优化运营线路，多建多分支线路、多交通线路共运。最后优化地铁票价，采用浮动票价、磁卡折扣、节假日优惠、游客票价等方式，将客流从时间上进行分流，缓解地铁运输压力。

Part II Your Turn

A. Role Play

Student A is a metro worker on duty. This morning, a large crowd of passengers are waiting on the platform. The train is not coming yet, but the number of passengers is still increasing. All passages and stairs are full of people. At that time, a train is coming. The passengers are crowded into the car, but the car is full. Is the accident expected to happen? What should you do?

Student B is a commuter who must take the metro to work. He or she gets up late today. If the train comes as usual, he or she will not be late for work. Now the train is coming, but he or she can't get on the train. What will he or she inquire the staff?

B. Reading Practice

Read the following passage and generalize the features of different metros.

Seoul Metro, South Korea

Seoul metro serving the Seoul Metropolitan Area is the longest metro system in the world. The total length of the route system extended as far as 940 km early in 2013. The first line of the metro was opened in 1974 and the system presently incorporates 17 lines (excluding the Uijeongbu **LRT** and the recently opened Yongin Ever Line).

The metro system is operated by multiple operators including the state-owned Seoul Metro, Seoul Metropolitan Rapid Transit Corporation, Korail, Incheon Transit Corporation, and other private rapid transit operators. Many extension projects are under construction on the already extensive metro network. The annual ridership of the metro system in 2012 was a **mammoth** 2.518 billion making it the second busiest metro system only next to Tokyo metro.

London Underground, the United Kingdom

London Underground, commonly known as the Tube, is the world's fourth longest metro system with a total route length of 402 km. It is also the oldest metro system in the world and has been operational since 1863. It comprises of 11 lines and 270 stations, and is operated by Transport for London (TfL).

The metro system provides inner-city metro services in Greater London and suburban railway services to some parts of Buckinghamshire, Hertfordshire and Essex counties. Surface lines comprise 54% of the system, while the remaining 46% runs on sub-surface and deep-level tube lines. The annual **ridership** of the system was estimated at 1.17 billion in 2012. TfL has been carrying out major improvement programmes on the London Underground since 2007.

New York Metro, the United States

The New York Metro is currently the world's fifth longest metro system, with a total route length of 368 km. The rapid transit system, serving the New York City, commenced operation in 1904. It is owned by the City of New York and operated by the New York City Transit Authority, a subsidiary of the Metropolitan Transportation Authority.

The metro system is operated with 24 lines and 468 stations, and is currently **touted** as having more stations than any other metro system. About 60% of the stations in the system are underground. The annual ridership of the metro in 2012 was 1.665 billion. Times Sq-42, followed by Grand Central-42 was the busiest station of the metro network with an annual ridership of 62 million.

Tokyo Metro, Japan

Tokyo metro system ranks the seventh among the world's longest metro systems. The total route length of the metro system as of 2013 was 310 km comprising of 13 lines and 290 stations. Private company Tokyo Metro operates 9 lines and 184 stations, whereas Tokyo Metropolitan Bureau of Transportation, also known as the Toei Metro, operates the remaining 4 lines and 106 stations.

Tokyo metro is the busiest metro system in the world and recorded an annual ridership of 3.102

billion in 2012. Since the opening of the first line in 1927, the Tokyo rapid transit system has been expanded to better serve the megacity with a population of over 35 million, and moreover, provides connections to suburban railway lines outside Central Tokyo.

Paris Metro, France

Paris Metro serving the French capital city Paris and the Paris Metropolitan Area is the world's tenth longest metro system with a total route length of 218 km. Paris Metro is one of the oldest urban transit systems in the world; the first line of the metro was opened in 1900.

Paris Metro consists of 16 lines and 300 stations, most of which are underground, and is operated by state-owned Régie Autonome des Transports Parisiens (RATP). Line 14 of the metro system, opened in 1998, is completely automated and driverless. Extensions of the Lines 4, 12 and 14 are currently under construction. The metro is operated with 700 train units and has an annual ridership of 1.524 billion (2012 estimate).

Words & Expressions

Seoul /səʊl/ *n.* 首尔（韩国首都）
LRT(Light Rail Transit) 轻轨交通
mammoth /ˈmæməθ/ *adj.* 巨大的；庞大的；艰巨的

ridership /ˈraɪdəʃɪp/ *n.* （某种公共交通工具的）客流量
tout /taʊt/ *v.* 标榜；吹嘘

M9-3

Discussion:

Please give a brief introduction of the following questions.

1. Features of Seoul Metro
2. Features of London Underground
3. Features of New York Metro
4. Features of Tokyo Metro
5. Features of Paris Metro

Unit 2
Safety Management Modes

What You Will Learn in This Unit

    1. General guidelines of safety management
    2. Basic requirements of safety management
    3. Operation modes of safety management

Part I Getting Started

1. The following chart shows the metro safety management mode. Do you know the exact meaning of different parts? Discuss with your partner or surf the Internet to find the answer.

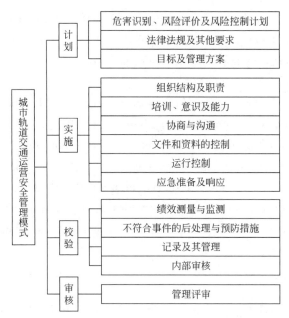

2. Do you think operation periods are more important than planning? Why or why not?

Part II Studying

A. Conversation

Mike was discussing with his students about the metro safety management mode in the class.

Mike: Today we will talk about the metro safety management mode. Can you list some parts of it? Jack, can you say something?

Jack: I think there should be planning and operation, because we must make some prediction about some possible accidents and then plan to solve them. Operation refers to the measures we should take during the accident.

Mike: Yes, you did a good job. We should do careful planning at first, in order to recognize the potential dangers and control the likely risks. The planning should be drafted by different departments with specific description. For example, how to deal with suicide-oriented persons on the railway, how to deal with the power cut, how to deal with the train broken or delayed, etc. Besides, in the operation process, the positions of different managers and staff members should be ensured. Each department must understand what they should do when the accident occurs. Actually, something more should also be considered. Who knows? Steven?

Steven: I'm not sure, Sir. Maybe after that there will be a check to see what we should improve next time.

Mike: Exactly. After accidents happen, there could be some problems or faults in the planning, such as the arrangements of the first-aid or hospital sending, the protection of the scene of accidents and comfort to the injured. Therefore, some adjustments should be made to update the planning. Besides, the investigation of accident reasons, process, and the result should be conducted immediately. All the materials should be taken down to make a report to higher hierarchies or bureaus like our authorities.

Students: Is that all?

Mike: Not yet. Logically, higher hierarchies will check the whole metro safety management and give some comments or suggestions on them.
Students: Oh, how complicated!
Mike: Yes, it's a process. At last, who can generalize the whole process again? Jenny?
Jenny: I've made some notes just now. I think there are four parts: planning, operation, check and leaders' suggestions. I'm not sure about the last part.
Mike: Oh, the last step should be audit. A-U-D-I-T, audit is to check the result from the higher department. That's all for today. Bye.
Students: Bye.

B. Words & Expressions

list /lɪst/ v. 列举；列于表上
prediction /prɪˈdɪkʃn/ n. 预言；预报
refer /rɪˈfɜː(r)/ v. 解释；参考；涉及；有关
measure /ˈmeʒə(r)/ n. 措施；量度标准
recognize /ˈrekəgnaɪz/ v. 认出；识别；正式承认
draft /drɑːft/ v. 起草；设计
process /ˈprəʊses/ n. 过程；程序；步骤
ensure /ɪnˈʃʊə(r)/ v. 确定；担保；保证
fault /fɔːlt/ n. 过错；毛病，故障
arrangement /əˈreɪndʒmənt/ v. 整理；安排；布置
protection /prəˈtekʃn/ n. 保护；防护
comfort /ˈkʌmfət/ v. 安慰；使缓和
adjustment /əˈdʒʌstmənt/ v. 调节；校正；改变……以适应
investigation /ɪnˌvestɪˈgeɪʃn/ n. 调查；研究
hierarchy /ˈhaɪərɑːki/ n. 层级；等级制度

bureau /ˈbjʊərəʊ/ n. 局；办公处
authority /ɔːˈθɒrəti/ n. 职权；当局；官方
logically /ˈlɒdʒɪkli/ adv. 有逻辑地，合乎逻辑地；合理地
comment /ˈkɒment/ n. 意见；评论
generalize /ˈdʒenərəlaɪz/ v. 归纳；推广；概括
audit /ˈɔːdɪt/ n. 审计；查账
safety management mode 安全管理模式
specific description 具体描述
power cut 断电
suicide-oriented 自杀倾向的
scene of accident 事故现场
the injured 受伤的人

Part III   Your Turn

A. What do the following pictures belong to in the metro safety management mode?

（1）_____   （2）_____

(3) _____

(4) _____

B. Speaking Practice

Scene A: A passenger fell down on the platform. Nobody accompanies him. You don't know what his problem is. Student A acts as the passenger and Student B acts as a staff member to solve the problem immediately.

Scene B: A passenger is chasing the metro, because his bag is stuck between the doors, but he can't get on the train. Student A is a staff member and Student B is the passenger. How should the staff member help the passenger to solve the problem?

C. Reading Practice

Some Findings of the FTA Probe to Metro's Safety Management

The federal safety management inspection of Metro included observations both grave and curious about the metro system.

Some passages of the report hit on issues already identified as concerns after a fatal Jan. 12 smoke incident in a tunnel just south of the L'Enfant Plaza Station: radio communications, ventilation and emergency response to Metro's rail operations control center, which monitors passengers and equipment maintenance on the lines.

Other passages offer insights into how things work—or don't—day in and day out.

A selection of findings from the report on the Washington Metropolitan Area Transit Authority, released on Wednesday, by the Federal Transit Administration:

• When Metro opened the Silver Line last summer, rail controllers did not receive a tour of the new line to see its **configuration**. Metro gave them a DVD to show the **alignment**.

• The controller desk that handles trains on the Blue/Orange/Silver Lines is nicknamed "The Monster" because it handles a disproportionate volume of calls and activities. But all of the controller desks handle a higher level of the activity compared to similar transit agencies.

• While federal inspectors were watching, assistant **superintendents** or superintendents at the rail center requested information from controllers by "yelling down" to their location. Also, as inspectors watched, shift **briefings** occurred "informally" as "coats were being put on and bags being gathered up to leave, with nothing formally written down or signed." Also, inspectors witnessed controllers using their cellphones while on duty.

• After rail accidents, Metro typically focuses its investigation on train operators but "generally does not look at the performance of the operations center or the individual [controllers]…" In "a few instances," Metro did not make sure that controllers involved in the incidents were taken for **mandatory** drug and alcohol tests.

• Controllers are supposed to be **recertified** every year, but that has not happened since 2012, which the report calls a "significant breach" in ensuring that they are proficient. There is also "very little" practice or simulation for emergencies, including tunnel fires or **derailments**.

• Metro is **short-staffed** at the control center, but veteran controllers **balk** at making hiring easier "due to the potential loss in overtime."

• There is a "significant number" of dead spots in WMATA's radio system, and despite some upgrades, "I can't hear you, Central" is a frequent radio transmission from the field. Many employees throughout the agency ranked poor radio performance as their top safety issue.

• Even when repairs to tunnel ventilation systems had been flagged as priorities, the repairs lagged. Two ventilation fans in WMATA's deepest tunnel location were locked out of operation for more than six months awaiting repair.

• Inspections of ventilation systems are documented on paper forms that supervisors must enter into an automated system, a process that requires "two or three weeks" and can **stall** work orders and reviews of critical information on the condition and performance of fans.

• Managers do not have strong enough assurances regarding the performance or quality of monthly inspections of fans.

• Metro has made "minimal changes" to its ventilation systems even as passenger loads have increased and eight-car trains move through tunnels and stations. Bringing the system fully up to current standards "would likely cost billions of dollars."

• Metro has trouble keeping maintenance materials in stock. In one example, the shortage of **brake pads** lasted more than three months and forced the **cannibalization** of brake pads from out-of-service rail cars and trucks.

• Replacing power cables "has largely stopped" after funding ran out, although after the Jan. 12 incident, a special program to inspect some cables in tunnel sections was announced.

• There is a lot of hurry-up-and-wait at Metro. Maintenance crews calling in to the control center sometimes wait "for hours" for the permission or verification they need for their work. Crews that have only 90 minutes to two hours overnight of actual track time face delays in getting clearances, which **erode** that limited time and enhance their safety worries.

In March, a crew replacing a bar that connects certain cables on the rail wasn't geared to get on the work site until 2 a.m. and had to start clearing out by 4 a.m. But the crew had brought the wrong size bar, specialized workers needed for the job were not at the site and there was confusion about whether there was proper planning for the task.

Before new parts and personnel could arrive, and the rail needed to be ready for morning passenger service, the original part went back in and no replacement occurred.

Words & Expressions

configuration /kən,fɪɡəˈreɪʃn/ n. 配置；结构；外形
alignment /əˈlaɪnmənt/ n. 队列；成直线；校准；结盟
superintendent /ˌsuːpərɪnˈtendənt/ n. 监督人；负责人；主管；指挥者
briefing /ˈbriːfɪŋ/ n. 简报；作战指示
mandatory /ˈmændətəri/ adj. 强制的；托管的；命令的
recertify /rɪˈsɜːtɪfaɪ/ v. 重新认证
derailment /dɪˈreɪlmənt/ n. （火车）脱轨

short-staffed /ˌʃɔːtˈstɑːft/ adj. 人手短缺的
balk /bɔːk/ v. 畏缩不前，犹豫；突然止步
stall /stɔːl/ v. 熄火；拖延（以赢得时间）
brake pad 刹车片
cannibalization /ˌkænɪbəlaɪˈzeɪʃn/ n. 为修配而拆用旧设备的部件；同型装配
erode /ɪˈrəʊd/ v. 腐蚀；侵蚀

M9-6

Tasks

1. Can you find any problems of metro management from the passages? Find them and underline the relevant problems in the passage.

Problem 1: Controllers using their cellphones while on duty.
Problem 2: The controller desk handles a lot of calls and activities.
Problem 3: A large number of dead spots in radio system, and they can't hear clearly.
Problem 4: Even when tunnel ventilation systems had reported to repair, the repairs lagged.
Problem 5: Replacing power cables has largely stopped because of the lack of money.

2. Consult the dictionary and totally understand the problems of management and make a comparison with our problems.

Unit 3
The Content of Metro Station Management

What You Will Learn in This Unit

1. Hierarchies of metro station management
2. Exact tasks of different positions
3. Train operation

Part I Getting Started

1. The following is the framework of metro station management. Can you write down the English names of the positions?
2. Do you know their different duties and responsibilities? Discuss with your classmates and present them in class.

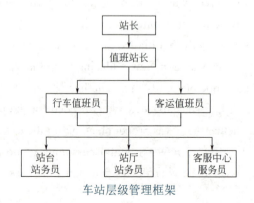

车站层级管理框架

Part II Studying

A. Conversation

The new attendants (NA) are getting a training course from their duty station manager, Sun Yu.

Sun Yu: Welcome to our station. Today we will learn some general rules and your responsibilities.

NA: Yes, Sir.

Sun Yu: You will be divided into three groups. The first group will serve in the customer service center. The second group will work in the lobby. The last group will work on the platform.

Sun Yu: The first group will mainly deal with the tickets. You should open and close the ticket center according to the regulation. While on duty, speak to the passengers politely, and give the correct change and tickets. Meanwhile, you should also answer passengers' any questions about the route, fare or charging the card in a polite manner. Check the invalid cards and solve the problems. Finish the weekly reports, and settle accounts and hand them over to the attendant on duty. Clean the ticket offices and lock the doors whenever you enter or get out of the ticket offices. Finally keep the fares locked up safely.

Group 1: Yes, we get it.

Sun Yu: Lobby attendants should pay attention to the ticket areas including the ticket offices and vending machines. If there's any breach of the regulation, you should try to prevent it in advance. Your main duty is to answer the passengers' questions and help them, especially the old, disabled, sick and children. Check the passengers who go through the side doors. Cooperate with the duty station manager. You should also check the floor or ask the cleaner to keep it tidy. Check the situation of escalators or elevators and ensure their operation. Notice and check the passengers with oversized luggage or some forbidden items, and explain the policy to them. Spot any drunkards or mental patients and prevent them from entering the station. You should be cautious of other potential incidents and report to the manager immediately once there could be.

Group 2: We are not very clear about our duties and can't remember all of them.

Sun Yu: No problem. Each one will get a brochure after class. You should read it carefully and learn it by heart before practice.

Sun Yu: The third group should be in charge of platform services. It's the most important part. You should keep the platform in order and inform the driver if there are any dangerous matters or persons. For example, someone fell off the platform. Check the safety of boarding and inform the driver when someone or something is stuck between doors. Stay in good cooperation with the driver. It's your duty to give the driver any immediate information needed and the driver should also respond to all your requests and requirements. Help the passengers and answer their questions.

Group 3: Yes, Sir.

B. Words & Expressions

responsibility /rɪˌspɒnsəˈbɪlətɪ/ *n.* 责任；负担；职责

divide /dɪˈvaɪd/ *v.* 分；划分

regulation /ˌregjuˈleɪʃn/ *n.* 规章；条例；规则；规定；管理

accurate /'ækjərət/ adj. 准确的；精确的；正确的
greeting /'gri:tɪŋ/ n. 问候
account /ə'kaʊnt/ n. 账目；账单；账户
breach /bri:tʃ/ n. 破坏；违反
overload /ˌəʊvə'ləʊd/ n. 超载，负荷过重
drunkard /'drʌŋkəd/ n. 酒鬼；醉汉
prevent /prɪ'vent/ v. 防止；制止；阻止
brochure /'brəʊʃə(r)/ n. 小册子
respond /rɪ'spɒnd/ v. 作答；回答；响应

in order 按顺序；适当的
duty station manager 值班站长
training course 培训课程
settle accounts 结清账目
general rule 总规则
hand over 交出；送交
mental patient 精神病人
be cautious of 小心；谨慎
be in charge of 负责；掌管

C. Notes

1. Opening Process

序号	责任人	内容
1	客运值班员	首班载客列车到站前 30 分钟完成车站 AFC 设备开启及功能测试
2	行车值班员	首列电客车出段前 30 分钟按规定完成实验道岔、安全门开关实验，组织人员检查线路出清情况，并及时报告行调（如施工工具、备品有无撤除等）
3	行车值班员	首班载客列车到达前 30 分钟，检查环控设备运行情况，首班载客列车到站前 15 分钟，打开照明开关
4	站台站务员	首班载客列车到站前 10 分钟领齐备品到岗
5	客运值班员	首班载客列车到站前 20 分钟巡视出入口，首班载客列车到站前 10 分钟完成开启出入口大门、电扶梯工作
6	值班站长	首班载客列车到站前 20 分钟巡视全站，重点检查站台及车站轨行区
7	行车值班员	向乘客广播候车的注意事项

2. Closing Process

序号	责任人	内容
1	行车值班员	末班车开出前 10 分钟开始广播
2	客运值班员	末班车开出前 5 分钟关闭 TVM，关闭进站自动检票机
3	行车值班员	末班车开出前 5 分钟，广播通知停止售票和进站检票
4	站台站务员	末班车开出前进行检查，确定站台乘客均已上车，无异常情况，末班车开出后负责将站台乘客请上站厅
5	客运值班员	末班车开出后负责站厅清站工作，关闭车站电扶梯和出入口
6	行车值班员	运营结束后，执行车站节电照明模式
7	值班站长	末班车到达前 5 分钟到站厅检查，确认所有 TVM、进站自动检票机已关闭，停止售票和进站检票广播播放
8	值班站长	检查清站情况，确认电扶梯、出入口关闭，照明转换为节电模式。关站后到票务室与客运值班员一起结账

Part III Your Turn

A. Speaking Practice

1. Get familiar to the process and make a report to your partner about what's your duty to opening and closing the station.

2. The following process is about the ticket selling. Match the process with English expressions.

（1）收取乘客购票的票款。

（2）讲出票款金额，重复乘客要求的购票张数和车票类型，如未听清乘客的要求，应主动礼貌地询问。

（3）检验钞票真伪，如钞票为伪钞，则要求乘客另换钞票。

（4）在BOM上选择相应功能键，处理车票，让乘客确认余额。

（5）清楚说出找零金额和车票张数，将车票和找零的零钱礼貌地一起交给乘客。

A. Here're your two tickets and your change, thank you.

B. Sorry, Sir, can you change another bill?

C. Madam, you want to charge 30 *yuan*, don't you? Please look at the screen and make sure the number.

D. Where do you want to go?... It's 4 *yuan*.

E. Sorry, Madam, I beg your pardon? Where do you want to go? How many tickets do you want to buy?

3. Do you know the following requirements for the metro staff? Discuss with your partner.

• Ability to make prudent and timely judgment in normal and emergency situations.

• Ability to maintain a neat and professional appearance at all times.

• Ability to speak clearly and distinctly in a pleasant voice.

• Ability to operate and service assigned station equipment as appropriate.

• Ability to furnish information with utmost tact.

• Ability to maintain a constant alertness to the overall station activities.

• Ability to interact effectively with large numbers of people.

• Ability to communicate effectively including orally (in English), in order to carry out duties and responsibilities.

B. Reading Practice

Job Description of Washington Metro's Station Manager

Position summary:

This is rapid rail transportation work of a moderately difficult nature. The employee in this job is responsible for monitoring and performing station services, assisting passengers in the use of station services and equipments, reporting to the Operation Control Center at any unusual occurrences, and providing assistance to public safety offices in the performance of their duties. The employee has **latitude** for independent judgment and action within established guidelines.

Duties:

Maintains observation of all public areas at the station, using CCTV equipment where required;

observes passenger flow through stations, being alert to unusual characteristics of patterns; assists passengers in negotiating the station/utilizing **Automatic Fare Collection(AFC) equipments**; makes announcements via the public address system to assist the public in the use of the transit system; and furnishes route information on such other assistance as may be required.

Monitors the operation of escalators/elevators through the use of annunciator panels and monitors the status of all fire detection equipment throughout the station.

Immediately reports to the Operations Control Center or concerned office any unusual occurrences, i.e., **vandalism**, public disturbances, AFC service requirements, equipment malfunctions, etc. complete written reports on all such occurrences and provides assistance to public safety officials (fire, police and rescue) in the performance of their duties.

Places fare collection equipment in-service and out-of-service as equipment conditions/passenger loads dictate; operates **reversible** passenger gates as required by passenger loads; and responds to problems indicated by AFC machine status display.

Overrides automatic gates opening signal if fire alarm does not require station evacuation; overrides date/time rejection if farecards have been incorrectly coded under previous emergency conditions; and permits pass holders to use service gate. Changes direction of station escalators to meet passenger flow demand.

Performs required duties and follows established administrative and operational procedures examples of which include the opening and closing of station and other gates/accesses; manual and automatic starting, stopping and reversing of escalators/elevators; and the servicing of AFC equipments.

Receives lost/found articles and turns in items in accordance with required procedure(s).

May work in variable hours.

Performs related duties as required.

Words & Expressions

latitude /'lætɪtjuːd/ n. 纬度；界限；活动范围
Automatic Fare Collection (AFC) equipment 自动收费设备
vandalism /'vændəlɪzəm/ n. 故意破坏他人（或公共）财物罪

reversible /rɪ'vɜːsəbəl/ adj. 可逆的；可撤销的；可反转的

M9-9

After reading, write T for true and F for false.

(　　) 1. Managers should go to the lobby to observe passenger flow through stations.

(　　) 2. Managers can make announcements via the public address system to help passengers use the transit system.

(　　) 3. Managers can handle all unusual occurrences to prevent them from happening.

(　　) 4. Managers can change the direction of station escalators to meet passenger flow demand.

(　　) 5. Managers should work in stable time to keep the station in order.

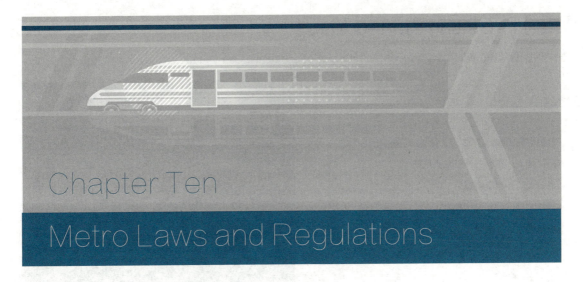

Chapter Ten
Metro Laws and Regulations

On completion of the module, you are supposed to:
1. Understand the classification of metro accidents
2. Know the rules of coping with metro accidents
3. Know the safe operation system
4. Understand metro emergency response plan

Overview of the Module

Safety is the most crucial factor in metro operation. The constant metro incidents and accidents have aroused a great concern of the public. In this case, it's urgent for the metro staff to totally understand metro laws and regulations so as to take precaution in particular condition and serve the passengers properly.

Firstly, the classification of metro accidents can provide all staff with a clear understanding of Chinese Railway Traffic Accident Law and help them realize the seriousness of the accidents.

Besides, learning the rules and regulations on dealing with the accidents can effectively decrease the damage. Meanwhile, it will help all staff stay alert to any emergent affairs and enhance their accountability.

The whole operation system can be smoothly operated, which depends on the cooperation of all staff and right handling of the train. For this, metro staff must understand the whole system and maintain their own roles.

In general, prevention is better than cure. Only when metro staff is all aware of the importance of safe regulations and precautions can the metro system run successfully.

Unit 1
Classification of Metro Accidents

What You Will Learn in This Unit
1. Classification of Metro accidents
2. Criteria for classification

Part I Getting Started

1. The following cases are different types of accidents. Can you classify them in English?

发生时间：2013 年 2 月 3 日 20 时 29 分
发生地点：东直门至三元桥区间
事故类型：列车救援
事故定性：A 类一般事故
事故影响：造成停运 7 列，到晚 5 分以上 2 列，调表 6 个。

发生时间：2011 年 2 月 29 日 6 时 34 分
发生地点：知春路
事故类型：电梯冒烟
事故定性：险性事故
事故影响：换乘通道封闭，电梯部分设备烧毁。

发生时间：2013 年 4 月 8 日 6 时 35 分
发生地点：苹果园站台上行车尾处
事故类型：列车刮蹭光缆事故
事故定性：险性事故
事故影响：停运 9 列，到晚 5 分以上 12 列，调整清人回段 3 列，中途折返 2 列，调表 58 个；5 组列车受流器受损；3 根通信传输光缆被刮断，52#站、53#站 ATS 脱机，调度电话、自动电话不通。

2. The following are classification of metro accidents. Do you know all of them? After reading, you should make a judgment about the following accidents and decide what kinds of accidents they are?

轨道交通事故分为特别重大事故、重大事故、大事故、险性事故、一般事故和事故苗子。	
特别重大事故	1. 乘客人身死亡 30 人及以上； 2. 社会影响特别恶劣； 3. 经济损失特别重大，直接经济损失 1000 万元以上
重大事故	1. 轨道交通发生爆炸、化学恐怖袭击等人为破坏事件； 2. 发生二级以上火灾（被困人数 500 人以上）事件； 3. 乘客人身死亡 10~29 人，或死伤 50 人以上； 4. 轨道交通运营中断 6 小时以上； 5. 直接经济损失 500 万元以上

续表

大事故	1. 轨道交通发生二级火灾（被困人数500人以下）； 2. 死亡3~9人，或死伤10~49人； 3. 轨道交通运营中断3~6小时； 4. 直接经济损失100万~500万元
险性事故	在地铁运营工作中，凡事故性质严重，但未造成损害后果或损害后果不构成大事故及其以上的事故且符合下列条件之一时： 1. 运营线列车冲突； 2. 运营线列车脱轨； 3. 运营线列车分离； 4. 列车冒进禁行信号； 5. 未经允许列车载客进入非运营线； 6. 列车反方向运行未经引导自行进站； 7. 列车擅自退行； 8. 列车、车辆溜走； 9. 列车运行中擅自切除车载安全防护装置； 10. 列车错开车门； 11. 列车未关闭车门行车； 12. 列车运行中开启车门； 13. 列车夹人行车； 14. 列车运行中，齿轮箱吊挂装置、关节轴承销轴、空压机、牵引电机等车辆重要部件脱落； 15. 电话闭塞、出站信号故障时无凭证发车； 16. 擅自向未具备封锁条件的区间接发列车或擅自向封闭区间接发列车； 17. 未办或错办闭塞接发列车； 18. 行车或电力指挥通信联络系统中断； 19. 信号升级显示； 20. 供电系统操作中发生错送点、漏停电； 21. 运营中车站照明全部熄灭； 22. 给水干管位移、侵限、爆裂跑水； 23. 排水不畅，积水漫过道床； 24. 地铁排雨泵站设备故障，雨水不能排出，中断列车运行； 25. 运营中走行轨由轨头到轨底贯通断裂； 26. 运营线路几何尺寸超限； 27. 轨道线路发生胀轨跑道影响运营； 28. 擅自触动、位移站台电视监视车门设备，影响正常使用； 29. 未按规定撤除接地保护装置； 30. 漏检、漏修或维修不到位发生重大安全隐患，危及运营安全； 31. 其他（性质严重的运营故障、安全隐患，经地铁公司运营安全委员会认定，列入本项）
一般事故	在地铁运营工作中，造成下列后果之一，但损害后果不构成大事故、险性事故及其以上事故条件时： 1. 非运营线列车冲突； 2. 非运营线列车脱轨； 3. 非运营线列车分离； 4. 调车冒进信号； 5. 应停列车全列越过显示绿色灯光的出站信号机； 6. 应停列车在站通过； 7. 列车擅自在不具备条件的车站停车开启客室车门；

一般事故	8.漏乘造成列车车长未上车发车； 9.列车车辆未撤除防溜铁鞋或止轮器开车； 10.列车客室内或车站的设施、设备、器材松动脱落等异常情况，造成乘客受伤； 11.运营线列车车辆空气系统（空压机、风缸）安全装置失去作用造成破损爆裂； 12.车辆或车辆载物超出车辆轮廓限界； 13.中断运营正线行车每满20分钟时； 14.直接经济损失在1万元及以上； 15.出站信号在中心和车站同时失控或紧急关闭信号失控； 16.运营车站正常照明全部熄灭或侧正常照明全部熄灭； 17.各类设施、设备、器材、物资等侵入车辆接近限界； 18.线路检查维修不当，造成列车临时限速运行； 19.无特殊工种操作证操作特种设备、车辆； 20.漏报、误报重大安全隐患，危及运营安全； 21.其他（经地铁公司运营安全委员会认定的安全隐患及问题，列入本项）
事故苗子	在地铁运营工作中，发生或存在安全隐患，但其性质或损害后果不够成事故条件且符合下列条件之一： 1.列车救援； 2.在站应停列车部分冒进禁行信号机； 3.通过列车在站停车进行乘降作业； 4.列车夹物走车； 5.运行中列车超过规定的限制速度运行； 6.列车在终点站未经允许进行带人折返作业； 7.因对车辆故障隐患未查出、未彻底治理，造成盲目出库上线运行影响运营； 8.电动客车乘客报警装置作用不良； 9.列车司机与车长通话和指令装置同时失去作用； 10.车长或副司机在列车关门后起动时，未进行站车瞭望； 11.执乘中未按规定要求执行呼唤制度； 12.列车信号、通讯设备故障，未及时报修、修理； 13.车辆、设备人为责任破损，经济损失2000元以上； 14.车内行车备品不齐全； 15.错发、错收、错传或漏发、漏收、漏传行车命令； 16.因错办、漏办进路造成列车变更交路； 17.擅自变更作业计划或安排； 18.调度电话或电台无录音或录音丢失； 19.行车计算机系统监测功能无记录或记录丢失； 20.私自听取或打印行车记录资料； 21.漏开有关运营的技术设备； 22.各类机柜门、检查孔未按规定锁闭或设施固定不牢； 23.站台电视监控车门设备故障超过30分钟； 24.列车、车辆、设备、机房、班组或隧道内、车站内的站厅、站台、办公用房等处（含非运营区域）发生初期起火冒烟的险情； 25.设施、设备发生异常脱落，影响运营； 26.施工、检修、清扫设备影响运营； 27.电器、设备接线不符合安全规定； 28.手摇道岔超过30分钟； 29.轨道线路发生非正常临时更换钢轨；

事故苗子	30.供电系统操作中发生漏送点、错停电； 31.供电系统发生非正常单边供电； 32.车站或区间的主通风设备发生运行故障，造成功能失效； 33.车站出入通道的台阶或地面破损，影响乘客安全通行； 34.车站大门破损，致使失去防护作用； 35.非吸烟区域吸烟； 36.未按规定穿戴劳动防护用品； 37.站厅、车厢乘客须知及安全标志不安全； 38.作业现场安全标志不齐全或不规范； 39.未经审批许可擅自进行施工作业； 40.进入地铁施工未登记或作业完毕未注销； 41.在地铁线路上施工未认真落实安全措施，现场无甲方安全负责人； 42.应撤除的设施、设备、装置、器材、材料、物品、备品、标志等未及时撤除； 43.应急抢险救援预案不健全或不落实； 44.应急抢险救援器材、备品、工具不完善、状态不良或不能正确使用； 45.应急抢险救援演练不落实； 46.防火预案乃消防设施、设备、器材、工具、备品未配置或状态不良； 47.经检查发现的隐患问题未能按规定及时进行整治或整治不符合要求； 48.对安全隐患未落实监控措施或责任人； 49.单位安全隐患统计、分析、记录系统不健全； 50.安全重点（要害）部位、处所、设备未落实相关制度，没有检查记录、故障记录、维修记录或交接记录； 51.违反劳动纪律、规章制度、管理规定发生严重违章、违纪、违制、失职、脱岗、当班饮酒、岗位打牌等； 52.安全运营生产责任制或安全管理制度、档案、台账不健全或不完善； 53.安全运营生产规章制度或安全操作规程未制定或制定不完善或不落实； 54.其他（经地铁公司运营安全委员会认定的其他安全问题和隐患，列入本项）

Accidents

（1）据××报官方微博消息，多名网友晚间爆料称，19时许，地铁5号线惠新西街南口站一名女孩被夹在安全门和地铁门中间，当场死亡。

（2）27日下午两点半左右，上海地铁10号线由于新天地站信号故障，在改用人工调度后，导致豫园路站两辆列车相撞。短短不到2个月，上海地铁再次发生信号故障事故。

（3）自动扶梯突然"倒带"：致一死三十伤。

内容来源：新民晚报

[2011年7月6日15:13]

转瞬之间，一位少年生命戛然而止……7月5日北京地铁四号线动物园站出现自动扶梯安全事故，造成3人重伤、27人轻伤。

Part II　Studying

A．Conversations

Conversation 1

Li Hui hurried back to the dormitory. He met Jack on the way.

Li Hui: How terrible! Oh, my God.

M10-1

Jack: What's wrong?

Li Hui: I've just met an accident in the metro station. Terrible, terrible…

Jack: Calm down, please. Tell me what happened.

Li Hui: When I arrived at the platform and waited for the train, nothing unusual happened except a large crowd of people waiting in a long queue. When the train came, a lot of people began to get on the train. It's so crowded. Finally, I failed to get on the train, but I found a lady being stuck in the door. She was shouting and crying. We hurried to knock at the door and wanted to stop the train, but the train still started to move away without any notice. The woman must have been killed. It's unbelievable.

Jack: How can this happen? No staff member on watch stood out to warn the driver?

Li Hui: No. At least I didn't find any.

Jack: Take it easy, OK?

Li Hui: It's a nightmare. I can't forget the scene ever.

Jack: If you have trouble in sleeping at night, you can call me. I can chat with you no matter what time it is.

Li Hui: Thank you. I feel better now. Bye.

Jack: Bye.

Conversation 2

The fire scene began to unfold at about 6:30 p.m. when the Harlem Line train out of Grand Central Terminal struck the black Mercedes-Benz SUV at the narrow, two-lane Commerce Street crossing, causing an explosion that engulfed both the car and the train. NTSB (the National Transportation Safety Board) sets to investigate the tragic Valhalla train crash. NTSB has taken control of the train-SUV crash scene where 6 people were killed and 15 injured on Tuesday.

M10-2

Robert (NTSB board member): We intend to find out what caused this accident. Why was the car on the train tracks and what caused this accident to be so fatal for occupants of the train?

U.S. Sen Charles Schumer: The train was traveling at the speed of 58 miles an hour, which is within the 60 mph speed limit for that stretch of tracks. The investigation team consists of experts in fire science, signals and crossings, to name a few. The team will review events recorders that monitor the Metro-North train's speed and brakes.

U.S. Sen Charles Schumer: We will be documenting the wreckage. We have already asked for aerial footage. Members will be using special 3-D laser scanning devices to take images of the train and also attempt to get any available data from the SUV.

Retired NTSB investigator Russell Quimby: Could the engineer have avoided the collision? Probably not. It normally takes up to two or three seconds for an engineer to see (the car) and react. Time is everything, and depending on what movements he made, he might not have got any time to handle.

Passenger Bruno: I was on my iPhone when I heard a big bang, jolt … it was obvious that we hit something, and then we eventually came to a stop. The car was heavily damaged, especially toward the front, and filled with smoke "pretty quick". There was smoke, there was fire, there (were) people on the ground and what we tried to do was to force open the back door—it could not be opened—

and so we took the window, the emergency window, we ripped it out, we started getting people out … helping people come down, because it was a big drop. As people were getting off we were just moving away because it looked like it was just going to explode … It was in flames (and) eventually it exploded. I just feel guilty quite frankly that I got out and … I don't think everyone did.

B. Words & Expressions

nightmare /'naɪtmeə/ n. 梦魇；可怕的事物；噩梦
tragic /'trædʒɪk/ adj. 悲惨的；悲剧的
strike /straɪk/ v. 撞击；碰撞；打击
crossing /'krɒsɪŋ/ n. 十字路口；交叉点
explosion /ɪk'spləʊʒn/ n. 爆炸；爆发
engulf /ɪn'gʌlf/ v. 卷入；吸进
fatal /'feɪtl/ adj. 致命的
occupant /'ɒkjəpənt/ n. 乘坐者；占用者；使用者；居住者
mph(miles per hour) 每小时英里数
review /rɪ'vjuː/ v. 再检查；复审；回顾
event /ɪ'vent/ n. 事件；竞赛；结果
monitor /'mɒnɪtə/ v. 监控；监测 n. 监视器；管理装置
brake /breɪk/ n. 刹车；阻碍
document /'dɒkjʊmənt/ v. 证明；为……引证

wreckage /'rekɪdʒ/ n. 失事；破灭；破坏
jolt /dʒəʊlt/ n. 震动；颠簸；摇晃
guilty /'gɪltɪ/ adj. 感到内疚的；犯罪的；心虚的
frankly /'fræŋklɪ/ adv. 坦白地；真诚地
flame /fleɪm/ n. 火焰；火舌；热情
eventually /ɪ'ventʃʊəlɪ/ adv. 最后；终于
investigator /ɪn'vestɪgeɪtə(r)/ n. 调查者；研究者
speed limit 限速
two-lane 双车道
aerial footage 航拍镜头
take images of 拍照
attempt to 试图
rip out 扯掉

M10-3

C. Notes

1. Valhalla train crash：此次事故发生在2015年2月5日的美国。当时，一列火车迎面撞上一辆黑色奔驰车，导致奔驰车爆炸起火，火灾又引发了火车车头燃烧。此次事故共造成六人死亡，15人受伤。

2. Mercedes-Benz：世界著名的德国汽车品牌，被誉为"汽车的发明者"。

3. Grand Central Terminal：纽约中央火车站，位于美国曼哈顿中心，始建于1903年，1913年2月2日正式启用。纽约中央火车站是由美国铁路之王范德比尔特家族建造，是纽约著名的地标性建筑，也是一座公共艺术馆。它是世界上最大、美国最繁忙的火车站，同时它还是纽约铁路与地铁的交通中枢。

4. NTSB (the National Transportation Safety Board)：美国国家运输安全委员会，成立于1967年，总部设于华盛顿，是美国联邦政府的独立机关。专责于美国国内的航空、公路、铁道、水路及管线等事故的调查，有些危险性物质在运输时发生的外泄事故也会由此单位调查。因美国是世界上主要飞机制造国之一，因此NTSB常会以飞机制造国的身份受邀协助其他国家进行航空事故调查。NTSB由五个委员负责，其中一个主席，一个副主席，这五个委员由国会直接任命，主席由总统直接任命，四年一届，国会每年下拨给NTSB的款项为7000万美元。

5. 3-D laser scanning device：3D激光扫描仪。3D激光扫描仪能对物体进行高速高密度测量，输出三维点云（Point Cloud）供进一步后处理用。

Part III Your Turn

A. Speaking Practice

How can you deal with the following situations?

1. A fire took place in a dustbin near a foreign guest, and you noticed the smoke. What should you do?

2. A train didn't arrive on time, and many crowds began to complain about it. The platform was suddenly full of noise. What should you do?

B. Reading Practice

Read the passage and answer the questions that follow.

20 Dead, Scores Injured in Moscow Metro Crash

Moscow: Twenty people died and scores more were wounded after a train **derailed** in Moscow's packed metro during rush hour on Tuesday in the worst accident ever to hit one of the world's busiest metros.

Russian television described scenes of **chaos** and panic on the capital city's famed system, saying passengers fell like **dominoes** when the train travelling at 70 kilometres (over 40 miles) an hour braked abruptly and three carriages derailed and **crumpled.**

Rescue teams were combing through the **mangled** metal carriages in an attempt to **extricate** several bodies.

"I thought it was the end," one surviving passenger said on television. "We were trapped and only got out through a miracle."

"There were lots of injured. Various injuries: heads, legs."

President Vladimir Putin, who was on a trip to Brazil, ordered a criminal **probe** into the tragedy that put a huge strain on the city of some 12 million and **snarled** traffic on its notoriously **clogged** roads amid a heatwave.

Sirens wailed as dozens of ambulances rushed to help treat the wounded and helicopters buzzed overhead to evacuate those with serious injuries, AFP journalists said at the scene outside the Park Pobedy metro station in western Moscow.

Nineteen people **perished** at the scene and another passenger died of her injuries in hospital, a health ministry spokesman said.

In 14 of Moscow's hospitals, doctors fought to save the lives of severely injured passengers.

In all, nearly 130 people were hospitalised and 42 were in serious condition.

The head of the Russian Orthodox Church, Patriarch Kirill, led a prayer to honour the victims, while city hall called for a day of mourning on Wednesday.

The accident raised calls for urgent improvements to the ornate but overcrowded metro, which first opened in 1935 under Stalin.

Words & Expressions

derail /dɪˈreɪl/ v. （火车）脱轨
chaos /ˈkeɪɒs/ n. 混乱，杂乱
dominoes /ˈdɒmɪnəʊz/ n. 多米诺骨牌（效应）
crumpled /ˈkrʌmpld/ adj. 褶皱的；弄皱的；（人倒地后）身体扭曲的
mangled /ˈmæŋɡld/ adj. 严重损毁的
extricate /ˈekstrɪkeɪt/ v. 使解脱；解救；使游离

probe /prəʊb/ v. 调查；探测；探查
n. 探针；调查
snarled /snɑː(r)ld/ adj. 纠缠不清的；混乱的
clogged /klɒɡd/ adj. 阻塞的；堵住的
perish /ˈperɪʃ/ v. 死亡；毁灭

M10-4

Questions

1. How many people died in the accident?
2. What happened to the train?
3. What measures were taken to deal with the tragedy?
4. What should the Russian government do in the future to prevent similar accidents from happening?

Unit 2
Traffic Accident Disposal

What You Will Learn in This Unit

1. First aid measures for metro fire
2. First aid measures for earthquake
3. First aid measures for metro explosion
4. First aid measures for power cut
5. Accident report process

Part I Getting Started

1. Can you analyze and say something about the causes of the following metro accidents in English? Write the names on the underlines.

(1) _____

(2) _____

Chapter Ten Metro Laws and Regulations 149

（3）＿＿＿＿＿＿＿＿＿＿＿＿＿＿＿＿＿＿　（4）＿＿＿＿＿＿＿＿＿＿＿＿＿＿＿＿＿＿

2. **Match the English sentences with the Chinese meanings and practice.**

Stay calm and keep quiet, please.	坐下，就坐在原地。
Keep away from the emergency door.	闪开！
Stand by for the injured.	此路不通／此门已经封闭。
Come here and follow me, please.	保持镇静，请安静！
Keep clear.	请不要站在紧急出口处。
Cover your mouth and nose with cloth or handkerchief.	请远离伤者。
The road/door was closed.	到这来，跟我走。
Sit down, just sit down.	用布或手帕掩住口鼻。

Part II Studying

A. Conversations

Conversation 1

Peter sensed a fierce shake and fell down on the metro floor. His head hit against the wall and was bleeding. He was struggling to stand up and found many passengers were injured.

Peter: What's going on?

Li Peng: Maybe it's an earthquake.

Peter: Oh, my God. We are in a big trouble.

Li Peng: Yes, we seem to be in a tunnel. What? The power is off.

Peter: I'm considering if there's someone who knows we are here.

M10-5

The passengers were shouting and crying. Some had lost senses and tried to break the window. 5 minutes later, some persons were running towards them.

SM: All passengers calm down, please. There's an earthquake just now. It's over. We are coming in to rescue you. (*In a loudspeaker.*)

SM: Please stand clear from the emergency door. I will open it from outside. Passengers, don't push, just wait for our guide. Just sit down. Sit down.

Peter: We are saved.

SM: Follow me to the gate and stay away from the injured. The doctors and nurses are coming. Everything will be fine. Please calm down.

SM: This way, follow me and follow my torch.

The passengers followed the staff to exit the tunnel.

Conversation 2

Yesterday afternoon a fire drill took place in Line 4 of the Wuhan Metro. A lot of passengers were emergently dispersed and other departments also took part in the fire drill, including a fire brigade, police, a medical team and other public transportation systems. The fire was controlled within 15 minutes and all participants were safely scattered.

A Metro staff member on the platform: There's a fire on the platform.

He immediately tried to put out the fire with a fire distinguisher, but it was useless. In that case, he immediately called 119 and reported to the Controlling Center by an emergency phone.

The announcement was broadcasted a minute later: Dear passengers, there's a fire on Platform 4. Please immediately leave the platform by stairs orderly. Follow the direction of the staff. Thank you for your cooperation.

All the passengers were shocked by the announcement and hurried away. Immediately the metro station was full of shouting, crying and quarrelling. During the chaos, the metro staff were showing big signs and holding a loudspeaker to help the passengers find the exit and move out. At the same time all escalators were adjusted to carry passengers upstairs. All bars on the turnstiles were down, and the passengers could smoothly pass the gate. After around 4 minutes, 350 passengers were cleared off.

The leader of the fire brigade: All firefighters get into the Platform 4 and search the injured and manage to control the fire at once.

After getting the order, the firefighters went onto the platform and did a search. At last, they found an injured lady, placed her on a stretcher and immediately sent her to the ambulance waiting outside.

After 10 minutes, the fire brigade assured the fire was distinguished, smoke cleared off, passengers dispersed and rescue mission completed.

Deputy General Manager of the Wuhan Metro concluded: Automatic smoke detectors are installed everywhere. If only it detected the fire, the fire automatic alarm system would be turned on. The system will open all the turnstiles and ease the passengers' evacuation. Meanwhile the fire pump will work automatically. The gas distinguishing system will be turned on to make the fire lose oxygen to prevent continual burning. The emergency announcement will be broadcasted on a loop, and the electronic screen will show red warning sign.

The fire drill was successfully finished within 20 minutes.

B. Words & Expressions

fierce /fɪəs/ *adj.* 猛烈的；凶猛的
loudspeaker /ˌlaʊd'spiːkə(r)/ *n.* 扩音器；喇叭
torch /tɔːtʃ/ *n.* 手电筒；火炬，火把
disperse /dɪ'spɜːs/ *v.* 分散，散开
participant /pɑː'tɪsɪpənt/ *n.* 参与者；参加者

adjust /ə'dʒʌst/ *v.* 调节；校正；改变……以适应
bar /bɑː/ *n.* 障碍；棒；横杠；条状物

firefighter /ˈfaɪəˌfaɪtə(r)/ *n.* 消防队员
stretcher /ˈstretʃə/ *n.* 担架；延伸器
assure /əˈʃʊə/ *v.* 向……保证；担保；使确定
conclude /kənˈkluːd/ *v.* 做总结；结束；推断
detector /dɪˈtektə/ *n.* 探测器；侦察器
oxygen /ˈɒksɪdʒən/ *n.* 氧
hit against 碰撞
lose sense 失去知觉；昏迷
fire drill 消防演习
take place 发生
rescue mission 救援任务

fire brigade 消防队
medical team 医疗队
Deputy General Manager 副总经理
automatic smoke detector 烟雾自动监视器
fire automatic alarm system 火灾自动报警系统
fire pump 消防水泵
gas distinguishing system 气体识别系统
emergency announcement 紧急通知；紧急播报
on a loop 循环；重复
electronic screen 电子显示屏
red warning sign 红色警示标志

C. Notes

1. 火灾应急响应措施

（1）城市地铁企业要制定完善的消防预案，针对不同车站、列车运行的不同状态以及消防重点部位制定具体的火灾应急响应预案。

（2）贯彻"救人第一，救人与灭火同步进行"的原则，积极施救。

（3）处置火灾事件应坚持快速反应原则，做到反应快、报告快、处置快，把握起火初期的关键时间，把损失控制在最低程度。

（4）火灾发生后，工作人员应立即向"119"、"110"报告。同时组织做好乘客的疏散、救护工作，积极开展灭火自救工作。

（5）地铁企业事故灾难应急机构及市级地铁事故灾难应急机构，接到火灾报告后应立即组织启动相应应急预案。

2. 地震应急响应措施

（1）地震灾害紧急处理原则：

a. 实行高度集中，统一指挥。各单位、各部门要听从事发地省、直辖市人民政府指挥，各司其职，各负其责；b. 抓住主要矛盾，先救人、后救物，先抢救通信、供电等要害部门，后抢救一般设施。

（2）市级地铁事故灾难应急机构及地铁企业负责制定地震应急预案，做好应急物资的储备及管理工作。

（3）发布破坏性地震预报后，即进入临震应急状态。省级人民政府建设主管部门采取相应措施：

a. 根据震情发展和工程设施情况，发布避震通知，必要时停止运营和施工，组织避震疏散；b. 对有关工程和设备采取紧急抗震加固等保护措施；c. 检查抢险救灾的准备工作；d. 及时准确通报地震信息，保证正常工作秩序。

（4）地震发生时，省级人民政府建设主管部门及时将灾情报有关部门，同时做好乘客疏散和地铁设备、设施保护工作。

（5）地铁企业事故灾难应急机构及市级地铁事故灾难应急机构，接到地震报告后应立即组织启动相应应急预案。

3. 地铁爆炸应急响应措施

（1）迅速反应，及时报告，密切配合，全力以赴疏散乘客、排除险情，尽快恢复运营。

（2）地铁企业应针对地铁列车、地铁车站、地铁主变电站、地铁控制中心，以及地铁车辆段等重点防范部门制订防爆措施。

（3）地铁内发现的爆炸物品、可疑物品应由专业人员进行排除，任何非专业人员不得随意触动。

（4）地铁爆炸案件一旦发生，市级建设主管部门应立即报告当地公安部门、消防部门、卫生部门，组织开展调查处理和应急工作。

（5）地铁企业事故灾难应急机构及市级地铁事故灾难应急机构，接到爆炸报告后应立即组织启动相应应急预案。

4. 地铁大面积停电应急响应措施

（1）地铁企业应贯彻预防为主、防救结合的原则，重点做好日常安全供电保障工作，准备备用电源，防止停电事故发生。

（2）停电事故发生后，地铁企业要做好信息发布工作，做好乘客紧急疏散、安抚工作，协助做好地铁治安防护工作。

（3）供电部门在事故灾难发生后，应根据事故灾难性质、特点，立即实施事故灾难抢修、抢险有关预案，尽快恢复供电。

（4）地铁企业事故灾难应急机构及市级地铁事故灾难应急机构，接到停电报告后应立即组织启动相应应急预案。

Part III Your Turn

A. Speaking Practice

In this part, you will read a report process. Translate it into Chinese.

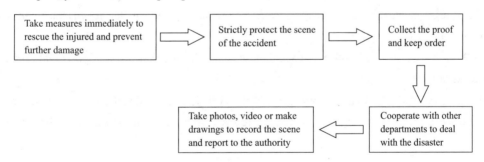

B. Writing Practice

Fill in the report form in English.

Accident Report

The name of the corporation:

Deputy of the corporation:

Telephone number:

Address:

Time of the accident:

Place:

Damage level:

Influence scale:

Total number of injured and dead:

Direct loss:

Describe the process in detail:

Others:

C. Reading Practice

Read the following news and answer the questions.

7 Killed in the Worst Accident in Washington Metro

Washington: At least seven passengers were killed and 76 injured when a Washington metro **rammed** into a stationary train on the same track during the evening rush hour in the "deadliest" accident in the metro transport system's 33-year history.

There was no immediate report of any Indian casualty in the accident. The impact of the crash was so powerful that the trailing train was left atop the first train.

The accident occurred last evening on an above-ground track between Fort Totten and Takoma Park close to the District of Columbia's **borderline** with the state of Maryland at 5 PM local time, throwing the country's second-largest Metro system out of gear.

Both the trains were on the same track, and one of them was stationary when the crash happened, John Catoe, Metro General Manager said.

A total of 76 people were treated for injuries at the scene, including two with life-threatening wounds, said Chief Dennis Rubin of the Fire and Emergency Medical Services Department for the District of Columbia.

Authorities put the death **toll** in the accident at seven. Earlier there were reports that nine people had been killed.

Washington Mayor Adrian Fenty described the collision as the deadliest in the metro system's 33-year history and emergency crews had switched to recovery operations after halting rescue efforts.

Words & Expressions

rammed /ræmd/ *adj.* 挤满了人的

borderline /ˈbɔːdəlaɪn/ *adj.* 临界的；边界的；所属不清 *n.* 边界线；边界

toll /təʊl/ *n.* 伤亡人数；通行费；代价；钟声

M10-8

Questions

1. When did the accident happen?
2. Can you guess the meaning of "atop"? What's the meaning?
3. How many people were injured and how many people were killed?

4. How many years did Washington metro system run?

5. Can you find some relevant news and analyze them?

Unit 3
Safe Operation System

What You Will Learn in This Unit

1. Four factors influencing safe operation

2. Metro Safe Evaluation System

Part I Getting Started

1. The following chart shows the metro safety evaluation system. Do you know what their specifications are?

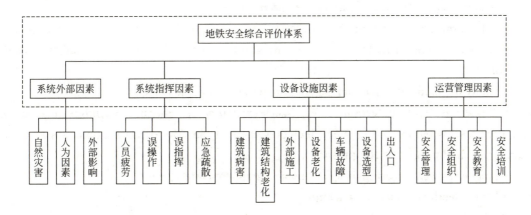

2. The following factors will influence the safe operation of metro. Please choose from the following table and write them down on the blanks.

bad weather   lack of organization   incomplete principles and regulations   electricity supply vehicles fire alarm system   lack of professional knowledge   violence   shortage of check inadequate order   little safety awareness   unclear duty   lack of flexibility   too much noise vending machines   irresponsibility   designing problems

Human risk factors: _____

Facility risk factors: _____

Environment risk factors: _____

Management risk factors: _____

Chapter Ten Metro Laws and Regulations

Part II Studying

A. Reading Passage

SUMMARY OF FEDERAL RAILROAD ADMINISTRATION SAFETY ASSESSMENT OF METRO NORTH

(**Excerpt**)

OVERARCHING CONCERNS

Overemphasis on On-Time Performance

• **Signal department** employees reported pressure from the **Operations Control Center** to rush when responding to **signal failures**. With the increased number of trains operating on Metro North, the time **allotted** to complete routine, federally-**mandated** signal testing was significantly reduced.

• **Track Department** employees said it was difficult for them to get the time needed to make necessary track repairs.

• When implementing the federally required operational testing program, testing officers reported that they did not **conduct** stop signal or restricted speed tests on the main track because of the priority given on-time performance.

Ineffective Safety Department and Poor Safety Culture

• A **disconnect** between Metro North's **safety department** and the railroad's **daily operations**;

• A lack of **communication** between the **safety department** and other **safety-critical departments**;

• **Safety department personnel** did not **observe** and correct **deficiencies** in the field;

• **Numerous**, easily **detectable** safety issues **existed** across **multiple disciplines** that should have been discovered by management, including the fact that Metro North employees were not wearing **personal protective equipment**;

• Employees were observed using cell phones **inappropriately**;

• **Poor attendance** at **safety briefings**.

An Ineffective Training Department

FRA found the overall training of Metro North employees to be "**inconsistent** and often **fragmented**". In response to the **retirements** of many experienced employees, the report said, Metro North hired approximately 700 new employees in 2013, and expects to hire approximately 800 new employees in 2014.

"An effective training program for new and existing employees with accurate documentation is critical for safe operations," the report said.

Yet, **FRA** found that while the training department is responsible for the overall training of railroad employees, it does not train all employees. Instead, "the training is fragmented across different departments."

SPECIFIC FRA FINDINGS

Track safety **suffered from**:

• inadequate supervision of the track program and inadequate training of **inspectors**;

- **the general state** of the railroad's track maintenance;
- the lack of time available to complete track inspections and repairs.

Railroad Operating Rules

Metro North did not comply with several federal **requirements** for operating trains over grade crossings under certain conditions.

Qualification and Certification of Engineers and Conductors
- testing and monitoring;
- **compliance with** stop signals;
- gaps in training;
- disorganized records.

Metro North also (1) did not train any of its testing officers on how to conduct operational testing, (2) did not have **documentation** regarding the required qualifications of each testing officer, and (3) failed to review its operational testing and accident data every six months.

Train Control Systems

Although Metro North has **extensive** and detailed signal standards, the **FRA** found it does not have a suitable recordkeeping system to ensure that inspections and tests are performed on time. In addition, the railroad **significantly** reduces the time allotted to the **signal department** to complete required inspections and tests.

Operation Control Center

The **FRA** found that (1) about half the workforce in Metro North's control center has less than three years' experience, (2) managers are not **formally** trained on how to perform operational testing for rail traffic controllers, and (3) there were no sound barriers between controllers or **chief dispatchers**, resulting in increased risk of controller **distraction**. The **FRA** identified fatigue as a possible risk area.

"Maintenance of Way" Fatigue

Investigators found that Metro North's practices increase maintenance of way workers' overtime, and along with it, the risk of fatigue and accidents. (Way workers build and maintain the tracks, bridges, buildings and other railroad structures.) Weekday and weekend overtime is common and sometimes extensive, the **FRA** reported. In addition, as of February 2014 Metro North had more than 100 **vacancies due to** retirement of maintenance of way employees.

B. Words & Expressions

excerpt /ˈeksɜːpt/ *n.* 摘录；引用
overemphasis /ˌəʊvə(r)ˈemfəsɪs/ *n.* 过分地强调
allot /əˈlɒt/ *v.* 分配；指派
mandate /ˈmændeɪt/ *n. & v.* 命令；要求；指令
conduct /kənˈdʌkt/ *v.* 引导；管理；指挥
ineffective /ˌɪnɪˈfektɪv/ *adj.* 无效的

disconnect /ˌdɪskəˈnekt/ *v.* 分离；切断；不相连
communication /kəˌmjuːnɪˈkeɪʃn/ *n.* 沟通；交通；通信
personnel /ˌpɜːsəˈnel/ *n.* 人员；职员

M10-9

observe /əbˈzɜːv/ v. 观察；遵守；注意到
deficiency /dɪˈfɪʃnsɪ/ n. 缺乏；不足
numerous /ˈnjuːmərəs/ adj. 很多的；多数的；数目众多的
detectable /dɪˈtektəbl/ adj. 可发觉的；可查明的
exist /ɪɡˈzɪst/ v. 存在；生存；生活
inappropriately /ˌɪnəˈprəʊprɪətli/ adv. 不适当地
inconsistent /ˌɪnkənˈsɪstənt/ adj. 不一致的；矛盾的
fragment /ˈfræɡmənt/ n. 碎片；片段 v. 使成碎片
retirement /rɪˈtaɪəmənt/ n. 退休；退役
inspector /ɪnˈspektə/ n. 检查员；巡视员
requirement /rɪˈkwaɪəmənt/ n. 需求；要求；必要条件
qualification /ˌkwɒlɪfɪˈkeɪʃn/ n. 资格；限制；条件
certification /ˌsɜːtɪfɪˈkeɪʃn/ n. 证明；鉴定
documentation /ˌdɒkjumenˈteɪʃn/ n. 证明文件；必备资料
extensive /ɪkˈstensɪv/ adj. 广的；多方面的；广泛的；大量的
significantly /sɪɡˈnɪfɪkəntli/ adv. 意味深长地；值得注目地

formally /ˈfɔːməli/ adv. 正式地；形式上
distraction /dɪˈstrækʃn/ n. 分心；分心的事物
vacancy /ˈveɪkənsi/ n. 空缺
Federal Railroad Administration （FRA）联邦铁路局
Operation Control Center 运营控制中心
Safety Assessment 安全评估
Safety Department 安全部门
Signal Department 信号部门
Track Department 轨道部门
On-Time Performance 准点运行
daily operation 每日运行
safety-critical department 安全核心部门
multiple disciplines 多学科；多规范
signal failure 无信号
personal protective equipment 个人防护设备
poor attendance 低出勤率
safety briefing 安全须知
suffer from 遭受；经历
general state 总体情况
compliance with 遵守
chief dispatcher 总调度员
due to 因为
overarching concern 全局考虑；全面考虑

C. Notes

1. Classification of staff risk factors

	风险类别	不安全行为表现
工作人员风险因素	专业素质	无证上岗
		应急演练不到位
		专业知识不过关
		操作不熟练
		工作经验不足
		教育培训不足
		操作失误
		临场应变能力差

续表

	风险类别	不安全行为表现
工作人员风险因素	心理素质	安全意识淡薄
		警惕性差
		注意力不集中
		责任心不强
		协调配合能力差
	生理素质	身体缺陷
		带病上岗
		超负荷作业

2. Classification of passenger risk factors

	风险类别	不安全行为表现
乘客风险因素	自身因素	安全意识差
		安全意识淡薄
		不遵守乘客守则
		应急能力差
	内部环境	设备、设施缺陷
		安全防护、警示标志不健全

3. Classification of equipment risk factors

	风险类别	物的不安全状态
设备设施风险因素	安全性能	设计不符合技术标准
		配置不够
		设备精度降低
		设备老化
	安全防护	操作规程错误
		缺少安全防护设施
		安全防护标志不健全
	维修保养	维修制度不健全
		维修配件不合格
		维修人员漏检漏修

4. Classification of environment risk factors

	风险类别	表现
环境风险因素	运营环境	清洁度差
		照明强弱不适
		噪声大
		温度、湿度不适
		通风条件差
	自然灾害	极端天气
		地质灾害
	人为破坏	治安事件或恐怖袭击

5. Classification of management risk factors

风险类别		表现
管理风险因素	规章制度	规章制度不完善
		机构职责不明确
		安全投入不足
		安全宣传教育不足
		应急救援不可靠
	运营组织	调度指挥不合理
		列车运行故障
		客运组织不到位

6. **Metro North:** The Metro-North Commuter Railroad（大都会北方通勤铁路）是由纽约大都会运输署运营的服务纽约周边地区的通勤地铁。在2014年该地铁每周运送旅客达298,900人次，是北美第二条最繁忙的通勤铁路线。

Part III   Your Turn

A. Writing Part

After reading the passage, please translate the following sentences into Chinese.

1) With the increased number of trains operating on Metro North, the time allotted to complete routine, federally-mandated signal testing was significantly reduced.

2) Track Department employees said it was difficult for them to get the time needed to make necessary track repairs.

3) There were no sound barriers between controllers or chief dispatchers, resulting in increased risk of controller distraction. The FRA identified fatigue as a possible risk area.

B. Speaking Part

Organize the risk factors in your department and discuss with your classmates. The following is an example.

In our Platform Department, I find there are some risks which should be concerned. For example, some passengers always try to push their way to get on board, especially in the rush hour. The flow of passengers is big. Many elders or the young might get injured in the crowd...

C. Reading Part

After reading, answer the following questions.

METRO NORTH SAFETY CONCERNS AND FRA'S SPECIFIC DIRECTED ACTIONS

The report directs Metro North to take specific actions to address each deficiency. We **outline** them below.

Track Safety Standards
- Create a plan for the use of advanced inspection technology.
- Ensure track is maintained to Metro North Track Standards.

• Collaborate with labor unions to increase the **availability** of **off-hours** maintenance time.

• Improve the training program for track inspection and maintenance.

• Analyze train schedules to determine whether there is sufficient time for inspection and maintenance of track.

Railroad Operating Rules

Change operating rules for operation of trains at grade crossings when certain conditions exist.

Qualifications and Certification of Engineers and Conductors

• Improve operational testing and inspections for operating crews.

• Conduct operational testing on main tracks.

• Improve the training program for locomotive engineers and conductors.

• Analyze event recorder data as a part of operational testing.

Railroad Workplace Safety

Improve the training program for roadway worker protection.

Train Control Systems

• Improve the training program for inspection and maintenance of signals.

• Analyze train schedules to determine whether there is sufficient time for inspection and maintenance of signals.

Worker Protection (Blue Signal Protection)

• Improve the training program for employees who maintain **rolling stock.**

• Ensure that blue signal protection is effective.

Operation Control Center

• Review and address risk for fatigue.

• **Mitigate** noise distractions.

• Improve the training program for employees who dispatch trains.

• Improve rules governing the use of panel blocking devices to ensure that they cannot be **inadvertently** removed.

Maintenance of Way Employee Fatigue

• Review and address risk for fatigue.

• Improve the training program for all maintenance of way employees, particularly track inspectors and supervisors.

Words & Expressions

outline /ˈaʊtlaɪn/ n.大纲；概要；轮廓 v.概述；显示……的轮廓

availability /əˌveɪləˈbɪləti/ n. 可用性；有效性；实用性

off-hour n. 非高峰时间；非工作时间

rolling stock 全部车辆

mitigate /ˈmɪtɪɡeɪt/ v. 缓和，减轻（痛苦）

inadvertently /ˌɪnədˈvɜːtntli/ adv. 无意地，不经意地

Questions

1. How can the organization keep track of safety? Can you paraphrase them into your language?

2. What's the meaning of "locomotive engineers and conductors"? Translate it into Chinese.

3. Who needs the training program? List all of them.

4. What measures can be taken to reduce the influence of the noise to the conductor?

5. Is the position of track inspectors important? Why?

Unit 4
Metro Emergency Response Plan

What You Will Learn in This Unit

1. Purpose of emergency response plan
2. Levels of emergency response plan
3. Different situations of emergency response plan

Part I Getting Started

1. Do you know the purpose of emergency preplan? Try to translate the following paragraph into Chinese and understand it.

In order to deal with the emergency in metro stations promptly, effectively, orderly, and appropriately, the authorities formulate the emergency preplan policy to avoid the expansion of accidents, largely reduce the casualties, and cut losses in property. It can also guarantee the safety of metro operation and maintain public order.

2. The following incidents will initiate emergency preplan. Put them into the right category.

earthquake   derailment accident   murder   riot   fire terrorism   accident   explosion   hijacking contagious disease   passenger surge   major power outage   typhoon   flood   landslide   poison gas biochemical attack   radiation contamination

natural disaster: _____
operational safety accident: _____
public health incident: _____
social security incident: _____

Part II Studying

A. Reading Material

SPECIFIC EMERGENCY RESPONSES

(Excerpt)

The **primary response agencies**, Douglas County Sheriff and Littleton Fire Department, are responsible for **initial response** and **assessment** of any situation. If requested, **District personnel** will support the primary response **agencies** as directed.

1. Flooding The release of water would **constitute** a major hazard to life, general health and **property** from the point of release at the north edge of Highlands Ranch and would impact heavily on Littleton, and other cities to the North. If early warning of a potential incident is necessary, the condition will be **determined** as follows:

– Flood Watch. Severe **upstream** or local flooding results from an **isolated** thunderstorm, rain, snow or general rain. One or more of the **detention** areas may be threatened by the flooding.

– Flood Warning. **Embankment** is partially or totally failing when the condition is without observing. (**Overtopping**, sudden increase in **seepage**, serious earthquake damage, large down-stream **slope slides**, serious piping through embankments, etc.)

–Flooding Underway. Heavy rains or failure of embankment have resulted in flooding. Homes and property may not be immediately threatened but **potential** exists.

• If the flooding occurs along **drainage** ways, trails heading into the flooded area should be closed and staff assigned to **enforce closure**. Additional staff shall enter the flooded area to look for victims in the flood zone.

• If flooding occurs in populated areas, perimeter security should be established. An outer **perimeter** to stop traffic on all access roads and a flexible inner perimeter along the **boundaries** of the floodwater. Personnel on the inner perimeter should be searching for victims in the flood zone.

• Condition Assessment Staff should be assigned to continually assess the status of flooding (is it rising or receding). Key bottlenecks, such as **culverts** across major roadways should be frequently checked to determine if **debris** may be **obstructing** culverts, which could create potential to overtop the road.

• Recovery and **Restoration** When the flooding has **subsided**, crews shall conduct a thorough **inspection** of all areas impacted by the event. Particular attention should be directed to all trail crossings, bridges, and culverts across roadways. Any significant erosion or degradation of the facilities should be noted for repair.

• Inspections should also be conducted on steep slopes along **drainage** ways and **outlets** from storm drain systems into the Open Space. In the event any damage may present a safety risk to the public, the area should be **secured** with the appropriate barrier such as fencing until the area can be stabilized.

2. Earthquake An earthquake in the area would produce two **extraordinary** conditions.

(1) Probable widespread damage.

(2) Probable lack of outside support from surrounding communities.

As a result, few specific guidelines can be developed for this type of situation. People normally staffing the metro should make every effort to respond—bringing food and extra clothing. Since there will probably be no specific incident area, command of the situation should be from the station or Controlling Center from the start.

- Initial Response
  – Contact **key staff** and return to ANY **District personnel** who can respond.
  – Check communication facilities to determine what are working.
  – If phones are in operation, establish a "hot line" for citizen information.
  – Announce location of emergency care and relocation sites that are established.
- Damage Assessment

Assign crews to conduct a thorough inspection of all areas impacted by the event. Particular attention should be directed to all District facilities that involve structures like park shelters, bridges, and restrooms, etc. Any significant damage should be noted for repair. In the event any damage presents a safety risk to the public, the area should be secured with the appropriate barrier such as fencing until the structure has been **stabilized**.

B. Words & Expressions

response /rɪ'spɒns/ n. 反应；响应；回答
agency /'eɪdʒənsi/ n. 经销商；代理；媒介
assessment /ə'sesmənt/ n. 估价；评价
flooding /'flʌdɪŋ/ n. 洪水；水灾
constitute /'kɒnstɪtjuːt/ v. 制定；组成；建立
property /'prɒpəti/ n. 财产
determine /dɪ'tɜːmɪn/ v. 决定；使决定；使下决心；确定
upstream /ʌp'striːm/ adj. 向上游的 adv. 向上游；逆流地
isolated /'aɪsəleɪtɪd/ adj. 孤立的；隔离的；分离的
detention /dɪ'tenʃn/ n. 滞留；拘留；延迟
embankment /ɪm'bæŋkmənt/ n. 路堤；堤防
overtop /ˌəʊvə'tɒp/ v. 高于；超出
seepage /'siːpɪdʒ/ n. 渗流；渗漏；渗液
slope /sləʊp/ n. 斜坡；倾斜；斜面
slide /slaɪd/ v. 滑动；滑；滑落
potential /pə'tenʃl/ adj. 有潜力的；潜在的；可能的
drainage /'dreɪnɪdʒ/ n. 排水
enforce /ɪn'fɔːs/ v. 强迫；强制；执行
closure /'kləʊʒə/ n. 关闭；结束；打烊；终止 v. 使终止

perimeter /pə'rɪmɪtə(r)/ n. 周长；周界
boundary /'baʊndəri/ n. 边界；分界线；界限；范围
culvert /'kʌlvət/ n. 阴沟；涵洞；地下电缆管道
debris /'debriː/ n. 碎片；残骸
obstruct /əb'strʌkt/ v. 阻隔；阻塞；妨碍
restoration /ˌrestə'reɪʃn/ n. 恢复；复位；归还
subside /səb'saɪd/ v. 退落；消失；消退
inspection /ɪn'spekʃn/ n. 检查；视察
outlet /'aʊtlet/ n. 出口；排气口；出水口；出路
secure /sɪ'kjʊə/ v. 把……弄牢；使安全
extraordinary /ɪk'strɔːdnri/ adj. 非常的；非凡的；特别的
stabilize /'steɪbəlaɪz/ v. 使稳定；使稳固；使稳定平衡
primary response agency 应急反应机构
District personnel 地区行政官员
initial response 第一反应
key staff 主要员工

C. Notes

1. City metro emergency response plan: 城市地铁应急预案，指面对地铁突发事件如自然灾害、重特大事故、环境公害以及人为破坏的应急管理、指挥、救援计划等。

2. Emergency response system:

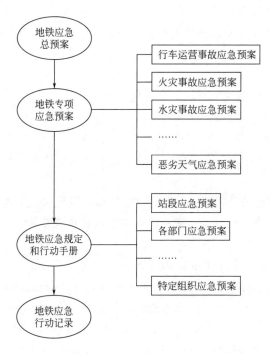

3. Emergency response for aid: 4. Reaction for metro emergency:

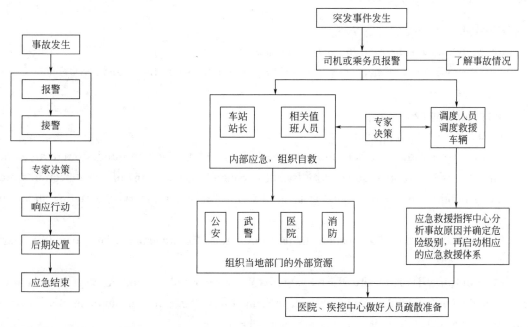

Part III Your Turn

A. Speaking Part

Read the following process of report for the accident. After reading, give an English report to your classmates. You may report as the sample below.

1. 报告人姓名、职务和单位（部门、车间、室）。

2. 事故发生类别、时间（时、分）、地点（站、厂、区间、线别、百米标、股道、车次号、车厢号、楼名、楼层、房号等）。

3. 事故发生概况、原因（若能初步判断）及影响运营程度。

4. 人员伤亡情况、设备设施损坏情况。

5. 已采取的措施。

6. 任何需要的援助（包括救援、救护、支援）。

7. 其他必须说明的内容及要求。

8. 向外部支援汇报时，应：

1）说明发生事件具体地点、人员伤亡情况，是否有人被困事发现场，如是火灾应说明燃烧物品及火势。

2）外部支援到事故现场后，应：告知其发生事故的准确位置；确认牵引电流或其他电源是否切断或隔离；确保各电器设备或行车不会对支援人员构成威胁。

Sample:

Hello, this is ×× speaking. I'm a staff in ×× Department. A fire (earthquake/flood...) happened in ×× Station at 12:20. The train from ×× to ×× was damaged in Tunnel ××. No. ××

The incident caused one car to be in flames and the train to be stopped. At least ×× passengers were blocked in the car. There're some injuries. Car No. ×× was on fire. I had tried to open the emergency door, but it's jammed. I need help from fire brigade and medical service immediately. Now I will try to cut off the power. ...

B. Reading Passage

Read the following passage and answer the questions.

Recommended Emergency Preparedness Guidelines for Rail Transit Systems (Excerpt)

Support Equipment and Systems

1. Fire Protection Equipment

A. **Fire Detection.** When trains are parked in isolated underground storage areas not immediately visible to or frequented by transit personnel, some means of fire detection which activates an audible or visible signal at Central Control or other supervising station should be provided.

B. Fire Extinguishers. The location and user instructions for fire extinguishers should be clearly marked.

C. **Standpipe/Hydrant and Hose System.** When the standpipe and hose systems are used, they should **comply** with the requirements of the authorities. Standpipes should be located wherever possible on the side of the trainway opposite the third rail.

D. Other Support Equipment. Third rail power "testing" devices should be available for ensuring that the power is indeed cut off when requested.

2. **Intrusion Alarm.** In many cases, rail transit systems operate trains along a shared corridor. The rail transit track may be located adjacent to highways, along the center median of highways, or adjacent to freight/passenger railroads. Motor vehicle accidents or train derailments may thus intrude

on the transit track area and present serious hazards to train operators unaware that any problem exists. It is essential that both train operators and Central Control become immediately alerted when accidents cause intrusion into the transit track area. Consideration should be given to protection of the trainway by physical barriers or by some type of detection and alarm system.

3. Flammable and **Combustible** Liquid/Vapor Intrusion.   Accidental flammable liquid or vapor intrusion creates the potential for a serious fire or explosion resulting in damage to the trainway and/or injury to transit passengers and personnel.

4. Flood Protection.   The underground and surface trainway in many areas may be subject to water intrusion. In addition, storm water drainage may enter at portals and shafts. Drainage and pumping station components for flooding reduction should comply with the guidelines presented in traction power, with the following modifications: Primary drainage should be achieved through the use of proper road bed design and construction. Excessive water should drain into grates, carried in culverts to a pump. Pumping stations should be provided at low points throughout the trainway.

5. Traction Power are seen in Graphics.   Graphics are defined as the informational symbols indicating the location and use for crucial trainway facilities and equipment. They are essential in identifying emergency exits and routes, fire extinguishers, etc. This section presents guidelines for graphics used in and along the trainway.

— Location marker signs should be posted along the trainway which are highly visible to the train operator.

— Signs indicating the distance to and direction of the closest passenger station and emergency exits should be posted, especially in underground sections.

— Each emergency exit should be identified by a sign and a light, and include instructions for use.

— Consideration should be given to provide bilingual and/or pictograph signs as appropriate.

— Standardized emergency graphics should be used.

— Information signs should be located at decision points for maximum visibility.

6. Emergency Power.   In order to ensure the continued operation of such vital components as lighting ventilation systems and pumping stations, two options for furnishing uninterruptable power must be considered. One of these entails the use of dual controls, feeder cables, etc., to provide redundancy in case of failure in one component. The second option is to provide an alternate power source in case the normal power source become unavailable.

The following trainway components should be considered for connection to alternative power systems:

— Tunnel emergency lighting,

— All illuminated exit signs,

— Selected signs,

— Ventilation system (metro),

— Public address system,

— Fire alarm system.

Emergency power system components should be located so as to be protected from damage by water or by normal maintenance to adjacent equipments.

Words & Expressions

fire detection 火警探测
standpipe/hydrant and hose system 竖管、消火栓和软管系统
comply /kəmˈplaɪ/ v. 遵守；顺从；遵从
intrusion alarm 防窃报警器
combustible /kəmˈbʌstəbl/ adj. 可燃的；易燃的

Questions

1. What's the meaning of "fire detection"? What's the function of it?
2. Where should the hose system be installed? Why?
3. What is the intrusion alarm? Is it important? How come?
4. What should the metro station do to prevent flood?
5. What's the meaning of "graphics"? How can the metro staff use it in emergency?
6. What's the function of emergency power for the rescue?

附录 地铁附属设施及公共标志英语翻译一览表

序号	中文	英文
1	入口	Entrance
2	出口	Exit
3	紧急出口	Emergency Exit
4	电梯	Elevator/Lift
5	步行楼梯	Stairs
6	前台、服务台、接待	Reception
7	问讯处、咨询台	Information Desk
8	厕所、洗手间、卫生间	Toilet
9	男厕	Gents/Men
10	女厕	Ladies/Women
11	残疾人	Disabled
12	残疾人专用	Disabled Only/Wheelchair Users Only
13	无障碍设施	Wheelchair Accessible
14	地铁中途停靠站	Station
15	地铁终点站	Terminal
16	地铁换乘站	Metro Transfer Station
17	注意安全	CAUTION!
18	危险	DANGER!
19	危险：请勿靠近	Danger: Keep Away!
20	安全通道	Emergency Access
21	消防通道，请勿占用	Fire Exit. Keep Clear!
22	防洪通道，请勿占用	Flood Control Channel. Keep Clear!
23	禁止未成年人进入	Adults Only
24	禁止通过	No Passage
25	请节约用电	Please Save Electricity
26	请节约用水	Please Save Water /Do Not Waste Water
27	请随手关门	Keep Closed / Please close the door behind you.
28	请按顺序排队 / 请排队等候	Please Line Up
29	请爱护公共设施	Protect Public Facilities
30	请扶好站好	Please Use Handrails
31	请节约用纸	Do Not Waste Paper

续表

序号	中文	英文
32	请出示证件	Please Show Your ID Card
33	有电危险 请勿触摸	Danger: Electric Shock Risk!
34	火警 / 火情警报 / 火情警报设施	Fire Alarm
35	谨防扒窃	Beware of Pickpockets
36	注意防火	Fire Hazard Area
37	注意防火，请勿乱扔烟蒂	No Littering with Cigarette Butts
38	有害气体！注意安全	Danger: Poisonous Gas!
39	严禁明火 / 防止火灾	No Open Flame / No Naked Flame
40	营业时间 / 开放时间	Opening Hours / Business Hours
41	紧急疏散地	Dispersal Point
42	老年人、残疾人优先	Priority for the Senior and the Disabled
43	严禁携带易燃易爆等危险品（进站）	Dangerous Articles Prohibited
44	严禁攀登	No Climbing
45	严禁倚靠	Stand Clear / No Leaning
46	非机动车禁止入内	Motor Vehicles Only
47	禁止燃放烟花爆竹	Fireworks Prohibited
48	禁止携带易燃易爆物品	Inflammables & Explosives Strictly Prohibited
49	禁止吸烟 / 请勿吸烟	No Smoking
50	禁止人停留	No Lingering / No Loitering
51	暂停服务，临时关闭	Service Suspended / Temporarily Closed
52	电梯故障停运正在维修	Escalator under Repair
53	电梯维修暂停使用	Escalator Out of Service
54	暂停收款	Temporarily Closed
55	正在维修	Under Repair
56	正在检修，请您稍候	Wait. Maintenance in Progress
57	正在检修，请绕行	Detour. Maintenance in Progress
58	当心触电	Danger: High Voltage!
59	小心脚下 / 注意台阶 / 当心踏空	Mind Your Step
60	小心滑倒，小心地滑	Caution: Slippery Board! / Caution: Wet Floor!
61	小心碰头	Mind Your Head / Watch Your Head
62	小心玻璃	Caution: Glass!
63	请勿跨越	No Crossing

续表

序号	中文	英文
64	请勿随地吐痰	No Spitting
65	保持安静，禁止喧哗	Quiet Please / SILENCE
66	请勿触摸 / 请勿手扶	Hands Off
67	请在此等候	Wait Here
68	请勿摄像 / 请勿摄影	No Filming / No Video
69	请勿拍照	No Photography
70	请勿坐卧停留	No Loitering
71	请勿带宠物入内 / 严禁携带宠物	No Pet
72	请爱护公共财产	Protect Public Property
73	勿扔垃圾 / 请勿乱扔废弃物 / 勿乱扔杂物	No Littering
74	请勿乱动开关	Do Not Touch the Switch
75	请保管好随身物品	Please Take Care of Your Belongings
76	贵重物品请随身携带	Don't Leave Valuables Unattended
77	伸手出水	Automatic Tap
78	请绕行 / 车辆绕行	Detour / Vehicle By-Pass
79	拉门	Pull
80	推门	Push
81	安全疏散指示图 / 紧急疏散指示图	Evacuation Chart
82	火警电话 (119)	Fire Call 119 / Fire Alarm 119
83	紧急救护电话 (120)	First Aid Call 120
84	谢绝参观 / 游客止步	No Admittance / Out of Bounds
85	禁止摆卖	Vendors Prohibited
86	施工 (检修) 给您带来不便，请原谅	Work in Progress / Under repair, we apologize for any inconvenience.
87	上车请刷卡	Please Beep Your Card
88	行人绕行	No Through Route for Pedestrians / Pedestrians Detour
89	禁止跳下铁轨	Stay Clear of Tracks
90	请勿挤靠	Keep Clear of the Door / Please don't push or lean on the door.
91	注意安全，请勿靠近	Keep Away for Safety
92	当心夹手	Watch Your Hands
93	靠右站立，左侧疾行	Stand on Right. Pass on Left
94	请勿挤靠车门，以免发生危险	For your safety, please keep clear of the door.

序号	中文	英文
95	为了行车安全，请勿打扰司机	Do Not Distract the Driver
96	车内发生紧急情况时，请按按钮报警	Press Button in Emergency
97	按下红色按钮，绿灯亮时对准话筒报警	Press red button, wait for green light and speak into the microphone
98	设施服务时间	Service Hours
99	服务区域/服务区	Service Area
100	暂停售票	Ticket Window Temporarily Closed
101	请勿蹬踏	No Stamping
102	紧急情况击碎玻璃/紧急时击碎玻璃	Break Glass in Emergency
103	机场方向(建议加指示箭头)	To Airport
104	请您自觉接受行包安检	Please Have Your Luggage Checked
105	1米以下儿童须成人陪同乘坐	Children under 1 metre must be accompanied by adults
106	请自觉维护场内卫生/清洁	Please Keep the Area Clean / Do Not Litter
107	请遵守场内秩序	Please Keep Order
108	老幼乘梯需家人陪同	Seniors and Children Must be Accompanied
109	遇有火灾请勿用电梯	Do Not Use an Elevator in Case of Fire
110	乘此梯至地下停车场	Elevator to Basement Parking
111	由此上楼/下楼	Upstairs / Downstairs
112	由此至地铁站	To Metro Station
113	投诉电话/游客投诉电话	Complaints Hotline
114	机房重地，非公莫入	Machine Room. Staff Only
115	自动门	Automatic Door
116	电源	Power Supply
117	请勿将饮料带入车内	No Drinks Inside
118	乘梯须知：乘梯请注意安全，请站在黄线以内，儿童老人应有人领乘	Notice: Stand behind the Yellow Line. Children and seniors must be accompanied
119	警告：防火卷帘门请勿堆物。开关操作时请勿站人	Warning: Keep Everything Clear of the Automatic Fireproof Sliding Door. Stand Clear of Switches being Operated
120	应急照明灯	Emergency Light
121	灭火消防器材/灭火专用/消防设施	Fire Extinguisher
122	禁止吸烟、饮食、逗留	No smoking, eating, drinking or loitering
123	放射物品	Radioactive Materials
124	易燃物品	Inflammable Materials

序号	中文	英文
125	危险物品	Hazardous Substance
126	剧毒物品	Poisonous Substance
127	旅客进站口	Passenger Entrance
128	旅客出站口	Passenger Exit
129	饮水处	Drinking Water
130	疏散通道	Escape Route
131	紧急逃生工具 / 仅供紧急情况下使用	Emergency Use
132	消防栓 / 消火栓	Fire Hydrant
133	售票厅 / 售票口	Ticket Office / Ticket Window
134	候车室	Waiting Room
135	行李车 / 行李手推车	Luggage Cart / Luggage Trolley
136	运营线路	Lines in Operation
137	时刻表	Timetable
138	乘车须知	Passenger Notice
139	意见箱 / 意见簿	Suggestions & Complaints / Guests' Book
140	祝您旅途愉快	Have a Good Trip / Bon Voyage
141	欢迎您再来	You are always welcome
142	行李包安全检查	Luggage Safety Check
143	疫情检查站	Quarantine Office
144	禁运物品	Prohibited Articles
145	请您稍候	Please Wait
146	值班岗亭	Sentry Booth
147	值班站长室	Duty Office
148	地图	Map
149	无障碍售票口	Wheelchair Accessible
150	上午 × 点	× AM / am
151	下午 × 点	× PM / pm
152	学生票价	Student Price
153	儿童票价	Child Price
154	志愿者服务中心	Volunteers Service Centre
155	小件寄存处	Cloakroom / Hand Baggage
156	特色餐饮	Special Delicacies

续表

序号	中文	英文
157	民族特色街	Ethnic Culture Street
158	牌坊	Memorial Gateway
159	塔	Pagoda / Dagoba
160	宫、院	Palace
161	石桥	Stone Bridge
162	庙、寺、观、宫	Temple
163	亭、阁	Pavilion
164	廊	Corridor
165	步行街	Pedestrian Street
166	瀑布	Waterfall
167	博物馆	Museum
168	展览馆/陈列馆	Exhibition Hall / Exhibition Centre
169	美术馆/艺术馆	×××Museum of Fine Art / ×××Museum of Art
170	科技馆	×××Museum of Science and Technology
171	天文馆	Planetarium
172	风景名胜区	Scenic Attraction
173	非吸烟区	Non-Smoking Area
174	残疾人牵引车(升降平台)	Wheelchair Lift
175	残障顾客专用坡道	Step-Free Access
176	硬币兑换处	Coin Change
177	外币兑换处	Foreign Exchange
178	地下一层/二层/三层	B1/B2/B3
179	第×通道	Passage ×
180	快速通道	Express Lane
181	长途汽车站	Inter-City Bus Station
182	火车站	Railway Station
183	始发站	Departure Station
184	×××公交站	×××Bus Station / ×××Bus Stop
185	楼层索引	Building Directory
186	东/西/南/北	East / West / South / North
187	存包处	Deposit
188	取包处	Bag Claim

序号	中文	英文
189	手机充电处	Cellphone Recharging / Mobile Phone Recharging
190	大桥	Bridge
191	公路	Highway
192	立交	Interchange / Flyover
193	隧道	Tunnel
194	提供拐杖	Crutches Available
195	提供轮椅	Wheelchairs Available
196	免费	Free Admission
197	信用卡 / 借记卡支付	Credit / Debit Cards Accepted
198	谢谢合作	Thank You for Your Cooperation
199	×号线	Line ×
200	换乘站	Transfer / Interchange
201	×××号车站	Station ×××
202	本站首末车时间	First/Last Train from This Station
203	本线首末车时间	Schedule for First / Last Train of This Line
204	列车向×××方向行驶	This train is bound for ×××
205	列车将要进站，请您站在安全线以内候车	The train is approaching, please stand behind the yellow line.
206	下一站	Next Station
207	您在此	You Are Here
208	站长室	Station Master's Office
209	车站值班室	Duty Office
210	地铁线路图	Metro Map
211	×××站示意图	Map of ××× Station
212	×××站地面示意图	Map of ××× Area
213	车站服务设施位置图	Map of Station Service Facilities
214	此口为地铁出入口	Metro Exit / Entrance
215	列车运行间隔	Train Interval
216	逆时针方向扳动手柄90度	Turn Handle Counterclockwise 90 Degrees
217	手动开门	Open Door by Hand
218	通道禁止停留	Do Not Block Access
219	本车今日已消毒	Train Disinfected

续表

序号	中文	英文
220	IC 卡售卡充值	IC Card Vending and Recharging
221	IC 卡查询业务	IC Card Inquiry Service
222	IC 卡售卖点	IC Card Vendor
223	月票有效	Season Ticket Valid
224	月票无效	Season Ticket Invalid
225	自动查询机	Automatic Reader
226	公交换乘信息	Bus Transfer Information
227	请您当面点清票款	Please Check Your Change and Ticket
228	请您保管好小磁票,出站验票收回	Please Keep Your Magnetic Ticket for Exit
229	售卡充值机故障,请您去临站办理	Machine Out of Order. Please Go to the Nearest Station to Buy or Recharge IC Cards
230	刷卡设备故障,请您使用其他设备	Machine Out of Order. Please Use Other Ones
231	机房重地,乘客止步	Machine Room. No Admittance.
232	请有序出站	Please Exit in Order
233	欢迎光临,请选择画面上的按钮	Welcome! Please Select the Button on Screen
234	请投入现金,然后按下确认按钮	Please Insert Cash and Press Button

参考文献

[1] 崔立秋. 城市轨道交通运营安全管理模式研究[D]. 北京交通大学，2009.
[2] 胡晓嘉，顾保南等. 城市轨道交通运营管理模式研究[J]. 城市轨道交通研究，2002（4）：43-47.
[3] 韩豫. 城市轨道交通运营安全管理协同机制[J]. 东南大学学报（自然科学版），2012（1）：178-182.
[4] 刘佩. 巴塞罗那地铁设计与运营特点[J]. 都市快轨交通，2014（10）：114-119.
[5] 宋江云. 地铁"大跃进"隐忧[N]. 中国企业报，2011, 8, 5.
[6] 王雯. 中国地铁让人欢喜让人忧[N]. 中国企业报，2010, 4, 12.
[7] 夏玲音. 高铁见闻：数说中国地铁[J]. 观察者. 2014.
[8] 邢五丰. 地铁车站站场管理办法细则探讨[J]. 山西建筑，2014（6）：255-257.
[9] 谢正光. 北京地铁管理模式分析[J]. 中国铁路，2016（11）：19-23.
[10] 禹丹丹. 波士顿地铁线路布局及运营组织特点[J]. 都市快轨交通，2012（6）：115-119.
[11] 广州市语言文字工作委员会办公室. 公共场所通用标志的英文译法[M]. 广州：广州出版社，2016.
[12] 国家处置城市地铁事故灾难应急预案. 国务院. 2006.